PUBLISHED BY
Cedrus Corporation
P.O. Box 6188
San Pedro, CA 90734
United States

© Copyright 1990-2000 Cedrus Corporation.

All Rights Reserved. No part of the contents of this book may be reproduced or transmitted in any form or by any means without the written permission of the publisher.

ISBN 0-9661842-0-3

Printed and bound in the United States of America.

Cedrus is a registered trademark, and SuperLab and ViaPort are trademarks of Cedrus Corporation. All other products and brand names are trademarks of their respective holders.

Cedrus Corporation
P.O. Box 6188
San Pedro, California 90734
United States

Toll Free: 1-800-CEDRUS1 (800-233 7871)
Other: 1-310-548 9595
Email: superlab@cedrus.com
Web: http://www.cedrus.com

Table of Contents

INTRODUCTION   1

    About This Book   1

    Installing SuperLab LT   1

    Opening and Running an Experiment   2

    Developing Your Own Experiments   2

    Acknowledgments   3

THE EXPERIMENTS   5

    General Instructions for Running Sample Experiments   7

Perception and Attention   7
    Experiment 1 Allocation of attention in the visual field   7
    Experiment 2 How do the parietal lobes direct covert attention?Summaries   10
    Experiment 3 Attending to Color and Shape: The special role of location in selective visual processing   12
    Experiment 4 Accuracy of recognition for speech presented to the right and left ears   14
    Experiment 5 Studies of interference in serial verbal reactionsSummaries   15
    Experiment 6 A feature-integration theory of attention   18
    Experiment 7 Temporal integration and segregation of brief visual stimuli: patterns of correlation in time   20

Memory   23
    Experiment 8 Depth of processing and the retention of words   23
    Experiment 9 Mental processes revealed by reaction time experiments   25
    Experiment 10 Knowledge structures in the organization and retrieval of autobiographical memories   28

Perceptual Representation   29
    Experiment 11 Spontaneous imagery scanning in Mental extrapolation   29

Experiment 12 The effect of landmark features on mental rotation times 31
Experiment 13 The Rate of mental rotation of images: A test of a holistic analogue hypothesis 34
Experiment 14 Forest before trees: The precedence of global features in visual perception 37
Experiment 15 Proofreading Errors on the Word The : New Evidence on Reading Units 39

Representation of Meaning 41

Experiment 16 Priming in Item Recognition: The Organization of Propositions in Memory for Text 41
Experiment 17 Semantic distance and the verification of semantic relations 45
Experiment 18 The occurrence of clustering in the recall of randomly arranged associates 47
Experiment 19 An evaluation of alternative functional models of narrative schemata 48
Experiment 20 Remembering: A study in experimental and social psychology 51
Experiment 21 Context-independent and context-dependent information in concepts 53
Experiment 22 Facilitation in recognizing pairs of words: Evidence of a dependence between retrieval operations 54
Experiment 23 The organization and activation of orthographic knowledge in reading aloud 56
Experiment 24 A ROWS is a ROSE: Spelling, sound and reading 58

Reasoning 60
Experiment 25 Pragmatic reasoning schemas 60

THE COLLECTED DATA FILE 63

GLOSSARY 65

INDEX 69

Introduction

Welcome to SuperLab LT. This textbook combines seven experiments in psychology with a limited time version of SuperLab Pro that you can run for up to 5 months. By time-limiting the use of SuperLab Pro to one semester, Cedrus is able to make this leading experiment lab software affordable to students.

About This Book

This book consists of a description of each of the experiments included on the CD-ROM. Combined with the instructions below on how to install SuperLab LT and run an experiment, this is all you need to use the experiments included.

Installing SuperLab LT

SuperLab LT works with Windows 3.1, Windows 95, Windows NT, Mac OS 7, and Mac OS 8. To install on a Windows machine, insert the CD-ROM

To install SuperLab LT on a Windows computer:

1. Start Microsoft Windows.
2. Insert the SuperLab LT CD-ROM into your drive.
3. From the File menu in either the Program Manager or File Manager, choose Run.
4. Type d:\setup.
5. Press Enter.

The install program will run. Follow the on-screen instructions which prompt you for the optional components you'd like to install and the directory location.

The install program creates a file named "install.log" in your SuperLab directory. Keep this file; it is necessary if you want to uninstall SuperLab Pro at a later time.

To install SuperLab LT on a Macintosh computer:

1. Insert the SuperLab LT CD-ROM into your drive.
2. Copy the entire SuperLab LT folder into your hard disk.

Opening and Running an Experiment

To open an experiment, run SuperLab Pro:

1. Run SuperLab Pro.
2. Chose Open Favorites from the File menu. A dialog (screen) appears showing the list of experiments currently included in the book.
3. Select the experiment that you want to run and click on the Open button. SuperLab Pro will load the experiment.
4. From the Experiment menu, chose Run. A dialog appears. Select your options and click on the Run button.

This is all you need to know to open an experiment, run it, and collect data.

Developing Your Own Experiments

To develop your own experiments or modify the ones included on the CD-ROM, you need to learn how to use SuperLab Pro. The SuperLab Pro manual is included in its entirety on the CD-ROM in an electronic format called the Portable Document Format (PDF). To read the manual on the screen or print it, you need to install a program called Acrobat Reader. The appropriate installers for Acrobat Reader are included on your CD-ROM for the Macintosh, Windows 3.1 (16-bit), and Windows 95/98/NT (32-bit).

Generally, Acrobat Reader requires about 8 MB of memory to run and about 10 MB of space on your hard disk. Although we encourage you to familiarize yourself with SuperLab Pro, you only need the manual if you are going to build new experiments or modify an existing one.

Acknowledgments

This project required the contributions of many talented colleagues, friends, and undergraduate students. Ellen Rooney organized the review of the psychology textbook literature to help determine which studies to include in this book. Jay Trudeau, Wil Graves, and Sujith Vijayan helped to design and program some of the experiments. Stacy Birch provided valuable assistance to keep the project on track, requested original stimuli from researchers whose experiments may have been 20 years old, and searched for studies that were feasible for computer use. Neil Stillings and Mary Jo Rattermann gave sound advice about experiments and were willing to try out early versions of the book and software with some of their students. A special thanks goes to my wife, Jacqueline Chase, who believed in the project from the start, encouraged me, and helped to track down copyright permissions.

Finally, Ruthanna Gordon deserves the highest praise. Over the last two summers and during the fall of 1997, she has programmed most of the experiments in this book. Her care and dedication to this project have been exceptional. She has a great future ahead of her in the field of cognitive research.

The Experiments

Psychologists and cognitive scientists have invented many clever ways to investigate human thought processes. Most cognitive experiments have been performed in the last 30 years using simple tasks that can be recreated today using a computer. With this book, the CD-ROM, and a little imagination you will discover some of the experimental techniques researchers have developed to study a variety of mental functions and gain a better understanding of the research that has helped to define how the mind works.

This book has several uses. First, psychology students need first-hand, research experience. Reading textbook descriptions of experimental work often does not give you a clear understanding and working knowledge of the experiment being described. Having an opportunity to conduct the original experiment on yourself will make all the difference. Second, to learn how to design and conduct experiments, you need to study the work of those who have gone before you. To help you get started, we have included seven well known studies from the research literature. These experiments are taken from a broad range of cognitive research and provide some interesting examples of different experimental paradigms. All of these studies are well known and frequent cited in textbooks and the research literature. They were the pioneering studies of their day.

For each study we have attempted to provide a replication of the original experiment using the same stimuli and experimental procedures. In a few cases modifications have been required in order to use a computer to conduct the experiment or to allow a single subject to experience all experimental conditions. Usually one experiment is presented from each article, though the original study may have reported results from several experiments.

Each experiment is described in some detail with extensive quotes from the original article to provide you with some background about the purpose and hypotheses behind these studies. The original methods and our modifications are also reported. We hope that the combination of the experiment and a detailed description will make the primary research article easier to read. Working from original sources is the cornerstone of good research.

Table of Experiments

Perception and Attention

	Allocation	Eriksen and Yeh
	Covert	Posner, Walker, Friedrich & Rafal
	Selective	Tsal & Lavie
		Broadbent
	Effort	Stroop
	Feature Analysis	Treisman & Gelade
	Pattern Recognition	Dilollo, Hogben & Dixon

Memory

	Encoding	Craik & Tulving
	Recall	Sternberg
	Episodic/Semantic	Reiser, Black & Abelson

Perceptual Representation

	Mental Imagery	Fink & Pinker
	Mental Rotation	Hochberg & Gellman
		Pylyshyn
	Global Precedence	Navon
	Word Shape	Healy

Representation of Meaning

	Propositions	McKoon & Ratcliff
		Rips, Shoben & Smith
		Bousfield
	Schemata	Yekovich & Thornedyke
		Bartlett
	Concepts	Barsalou
	Lexical Organization	Meyer & Schvaneveldt
		Glushko
		Van Orden

Reasoning

		Cheng & Holyoak

SuperLab LT

General Instructions for Running Sample Experiments

You are encouraged to run each experiment using yourself as subject, collect your data, and then examine the results using whatever statistical or graphing program is available to your class. Your teacher may want to you to bring your data to class so that group averages and individual differences can be examined. After running yourself as a subject, try to answer the following questions:

1. What were the dependent and independent variables for this experiment?
2. What other potentially confounding factors were controlled for in this experiment and how?

Running these sample experiments is straightforward. See the instructions at the beginning of the book. Have fun.

Perception and Attention

Experiment 1
Allocation of attention in the visual field

Eriksen, C., & Yeh, Y. (1985). Allocation of attention in the visual field. Journal of Experimental Psychology: *Human Perception and Performance*, **11**, 583-597. Copyright (1985) by the American Psychological Association. Reprinted with permission.

Introduction

When you are searching for a face in a crowd, how do you direct and divide your attention? Previous research has supported variations on a two-stage model of attentional allocation. The first stage partially analyzes many faces at the same time or in parallel. But the capacity to analyze each face is limited. Not all the information is passed onto stage two. Depending on the model, Stage 2 is where you become consciously aware of the faces you have seen, where they enter short-term memory, or simply where they are analyzed in greater detail.

The authors here explore one such model proposed by Jonides (1983). In this model:

> Subjects have two modes of attending the visual display: (a) They can allocate attentional resources evenly across the entire display, processing the display elements in parallel but at a relatively slow rate; or (b) in response to a precue, they can concentrate attentional resources on one display location. In this second mode, processing is facilitated. (p.585)

The present experiment asks several questions:

> (a) Can attention be simultaneously focused on separate locations in the visual field? (b) When attention is prefocused on an invalid display location, does the system then revert to parallel search, or does serial search in the focal attentional mode continue over the other display locations? (c) When attention is focused, are there still some resources allocated to the non-focused locations? (d) What is the nature of the costs when attention is focused on an invalid location? (p.585)

Method Subjects were six undergraduate students with normal or corrected-to-normal vision. The visual display consisted of a circular arrangement of eight letters with a fixation point in the center that in the largest display subtended a viewing angle of 2 1/2 degrees. Subjects' task was to search for a target letter, S or Y, in the display. One or the other target appeared in the 12, 3, 6, or 9 o'clock position.

Subjects completed the search with the help of a visual cue. Four types of cues were used: a control condition without cueing, and conditions in which the precue indicated the target position with 40%, 70%, and 100% validity. For the 40% condition, the target was in the position diametrically opposite the precue 40% of the time as well; for the 70% condition it held that position 10% of the time. The use of such cues would help to determine whether subjects were using a serial or parallel search. All subjects ran in all conditions. They were told which condition each session was at the beginning of that session, and encouraged to make use of the information. Feedback was given on accuracy and reaction time.

Subject completed six sessions. The first was practice, followed by four sessions counter-balanced in order for each cue condition. The six session tested subjects on the 40% and 70% cues. Each session consisted of five blocks of 40 trials.

Results and Discussion There is a significant reduction in reaction time for the primary cued location. This reduction increases as the precue probability increases. The results are the opposite for the secondary cued location: performance is slower in the precue than in the control conditions, and worsens as probability increases. However, reaction time for the secondary position is better than for the two non-cued positions.

Significance was tested on three separate ANOVAs. A two-way classification (Subjects x control & validity conditions) found significance for control and validity conditions ($F = 24.69$, $p<.0001$). A similar analysis for the secondary location data also showed significance for validity condition ($F = 8.69$, $P<.005$). The third analysis compared the secondary and non-cued positions, confirming that the faster secondary performance was significant ($F = 12.82$, $p<.05$)

The authors conclude that the results of this experiment support Jonides' two-process model.

> In the present experiment we would interpret the subjects' performance under [the control condition] as reflecting the distributed resource mode of operation. Here the display positions are searched simultaneously and in parallel. In the experimental conditions where display locations are precued, the subjects vary their attentional approach to the task from trial to trial. Across trials they employ probability matching, using the focused approach roughly in proportion to the validity of the precue. (p.589)

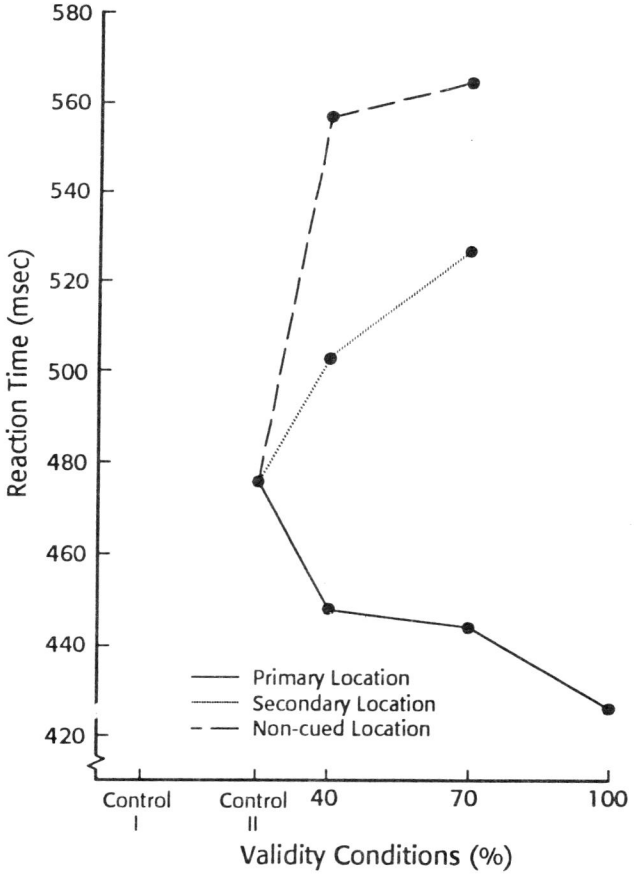

Figure 1. Response Latency (in msec) as a function of control and probability conditions for targets located in the primary cued location, the secondary cued location, and the average of the two noncued locations. The primary location is a position adjacent to the precue, whereas the secondary location is opposite the primary location. The noncue

location is average performance on trials with the target in the two remaining target locations.

Eriksen and Yeh suggested that subjects do not use the focused approach consistently due to the costs in reaction time when the cue is invalid.

Running the Experiment Eriksen and Yeh's first experiment is presented with the number of trials has been reduced to 40 in each condition.

Data Analysis Trials are coded for four variables: % accuracy, position, cue, and letter. % accuracy defines the accuracy of the cue (40%, 70%, and 100%). Position defines where the target appeared (north, east, south, or west). Cue defines its position (correct, opposite, or incorrect). Letter defines the target letter which appeared (S or Y).

References Cited Jonides, J. (1983). Further toward a model of the mind's eye's movement. *Bulletin of the Psychonomic Society*, **21**, 247-250.

Experiment 2
How do the parietal lobes direct covert attention?Summaries

Posner, M., Walker, J., Friedrich, F., & Rafal, R. (1987). How do the parietal lobes direct covert attention?Posner, M., Walker, J., Friedrich, F., & Rafal, R. (1987). How do the parietal lobes direct covert attention? *Neuropsychologia*, **25**, 135-145. Reprinted with permission from Elsevier Science.

Introduction Previous research has shown that patients with lesions to the posterior parietal lobe have difficulty disengaging their attention and refocusing it to a stimulus in the visual field opposite (contralateral to) the lesioned side.

> This paper attempts to determine whether lesions of the parietal lobe produce a deficit in shifting attention in a direction opposite to the lesion (contralesional) irrespective of the field in which the target occurs. Although deficits on the contralesional side of objects irrespective of visual field have been reported in clinical neurology theories of deficit found with parietal lesions have not usually seen this as a fundamental aspect of the disorder. (p.135)

Method Ten normal subjects, who were free of known neurological abnormalities, and seven patients with parietal lesions (verified by CT scan) resulting from strokes, were studied. All parietal lesioned patients showed problems with shifting their attention as indicated by "delayed RTs to stimuli in the contralateral field following central and ipsilateral [same-side] cues."

A sample trial is shown in figure 2.

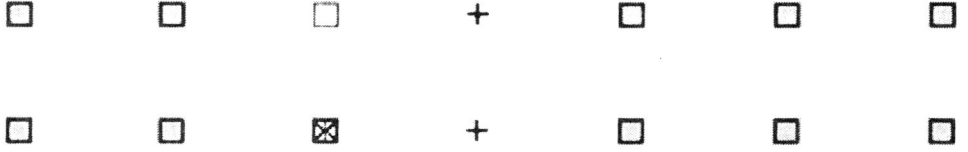

Figure 2. Valid cue followed by target.

> [In this paradigm] subjects fixate on a cross located at the center of a [screen]. Three boxes are present in each visual hemifield. Subjects are first cued to one of the six boxes by brightening of the box. A detection target is presented either at the cued location, at another location in the same visual field, or in the opposite field. The subject presses a single key whenever the target stimulus occurs. Reaction time to the target is the measure of efficiency of target detection. (p.135)

The three squares on each side were 3, 6, and 9 degrees away from the central fixation point. The cue consisted of one square brightening for 150 milliseconds. The target appeared as a cross in a square, either 100 or 600 milliseconds after cue onset. Forty percent of the trials were valid; that is, the target appeared in the same square as the cue. For all invalid trials the target appeared in the central square of one hemifield. Invalid trials were of three types: cross trials in which the target appeared in the hemifield opposite the cue, within-field trials in which the target was to the left of the cue (requiring leftward eye movement), and within-field trials in which the target was to the right of the cue (requiring rightward eye movement). There were a total of 300 trials.

Results and Discussion

Many different comparisons could be made. However, one condition is more critical than the others.

> The crucial comparisons involved trials in which there was a center target (6°) following one of the four types of cues (valid, cross, move left, move right). Separate ANOVA on normals and patients were run on these trials in which the variables were cue condition (valid, cross, move), visual field [left vs. right for normals and contra vs. ipsi for patients], and interval. (p.137)

Normals showed significant effects for cue-target interval (F=46.4, $p<.001$) and field by condition interaction (F=3.03, $p<.05$). Rightward movements of attention were faster in the left visual field, whereas leftward movements were faster in the right.

> One way to describe this interaction is to say that movements inward toward the fovea are faster than movements outward

> away from the fovea. Alternatively one could say that the more distant the cue is from the fovea the faster the response to center targets. (p. 138)

Patients showed significant effects for interval (F=33.5, $p<.001$), field (contra vs. ipsilesional) (F=23.2, $p<.003$), cue condition (F=16.3, $p<.001$), and field by cue condition (F=4.7, $p<.01$). Of particular interest to the hypothesis are the findings for eye movement direction on within-field trials:

> There is a significant main effect advantage for movements in the ipsilesional direction (leftward for patients with left lesions and rightward for patients with right lesions) when compared with movements in the contralesional direction (F=5.7, p<.05). ...The advantage of movements in the ipsilesional direction is greater in the contralateral field than in the ipsilateral field (F=5.6, p<.05). (p.139-140)

The authors conclude:

> The results of the experiment favor the idea that the direction of the attention shift is at least a major difficulty caused by the parietal lesion. (p.140)

Running the Experiment Posner's experiment one, which presumably will be performed by students without parietal lesions, eliminates between-subject comparisons. Students should still be able to demonstrate the hemispheric effects that were apparent for normal subjects. The experiment also has been shortened to 120 trials.

Data Analysis Each trial has three code values: condition, ISI, and visual field. The condition describes where the target was in relation to the cue: valid, cross, to the left, right or peripheral. The ISI defines the delay between the cue and target: 100 ms or 600 ms. The visual field defines where the target appears: left visual field or right.

Experiment 3
Attending to Color and Shape: The special role of location in selective visual processing

---

Tsal, Y., & Lavie, N. (1988). Attending to Color and Shape: The special role of location in selective visual processing. *Perception & Psychophysics,* **44**, 15-21. Reprinted by permission of Psychonomic Society, Inc.

Introduction Is location simply another property of a visual stimulus, like color and shape, or does it play a special role? Early theories of visual attention assumed that location is ignored unless it happens to be the relevant stimulus dimension to which attention is being directed. However, more recent studies have shown that advanced knowledge about the location of a target facilitates processing in that location. These results have led to a theory that attention "operates as a 'spotlight' that 'illuminates' a given small area within which stimuli are processed in detail." (p.15)

> In the present study we explored the possibility that attending to location is a general and mandatory process that is not restricted to tasks that precue the locus of a stimulus. Specifically, our purpose was to investigate whether attention is allocated to location even when this dimension is irrelevant to the task, that is, when the target is prespecified by color or by shape. (p.16)

Method   Subjects were ten undergraduates with normal or corrected to normal vision. Stimuli were 36 circular arrays of nine uppercase letters, none repeated in a given array. Eighteen were presented twice for a total of 54 trials. Each array had a diameter of 6.6 degrees of visual angle. Two of the letters were "curved" (selected from the set of: D, G, O, and Q), while the other seven were angular. On each trial, a fixation cross was presented for one second, and the stimulus for 100 ms. Subjects were to first report the name of one curved letter, and then any others they could identify.

Results and Discussion   After the first letter reported, the other letters in the display were categorized by location (letters adjacent to the first reported), shape (the other curved letter), or neutral (angular letters not adjacent to the first reported curved letter).

Location letters were reported more frequently than neutral letters (p<.005), but there was no significant difference between location and shape letters. These results suggest that a subject's attention is directed by location, regardless of what visual property they are searching for.

Running the Experiment   Tsal and Lavie's second experiment is presented here. The study requires free recall, so you will need a piece of paper and a pen to record your answers.

Data Analysis   The data file will contain multiple responses for each trial. The error codes for these responses are not accurate, but the responses are accurate and record in order which letters the subject reported seeing on a trial. The last response for each trial will have an "SC" error code. In the data file are trial codes which report which letters were present in the display. The four targets (D, O, G, and Q) are defined as present or absent. The other letters used (A, E, F, H, I, K, L, M, N, T, V, W, X, Y, Z) are defined as adjacent, neutral, or absent.

To complete the analysis, a subject's data needs to be recoded and checked for accuracy. First, each letter reported needs to be checked for accuracy. Was it present in the display? Then letters which are accurately reported need to be categorized into one of three types: location (a letter adjacent to one of the curved letters first reported, shape (the other curved letter), or neutral (angular letters which are not adjacent to the first reported curved letter). Statistical analysis then can be completed on the mean number of letters per trial correctly reported in each category in addition to the first curved target letter.

Experiment 4
Accuracy of recognition for speech presented to the right and left ears

---

Broadbent, D.E. & Gregory, M. (1963). Accuracy of recognition for speech presented to the right and left ears. *Quarterly Journal of Experimental Psychology*, 16, 359-360. Reprinted by permission of the Experimental Psychology Society.

Introduction Dichotic listening, the presentation of different sounds to each ear, is now a well known experimental procedure used to study and localize cognitive functions to different brain hemispheres. In their first experiments, Broadbent and Kimura found that subjects are more likely to recall words presented to the right ear over the left ear. However, a similar experiment with music found a left ear advantage (LEA) using a recognition tests. Since the right ear advantage (REA) for words was based on a recall test, it is possible that the difference resulted from the method rather than material type. Broadbent designed this experiment to use a recognition test with spoken words in order to determine if the REA is based on the task or the type of sound.

Method Subjects were 18 men between the ages of 18 and 30. On each of 24 trials, subjects were first presented with a triad of numbers in each ear. Each pair of digits arrived simultaneously. Each pair of triads shared one digit, but the repeated digit did not appear in the same position. This was followed by four groups of three digits, from which the subject was required to pick the two heard. An example is shown in Figure 3:

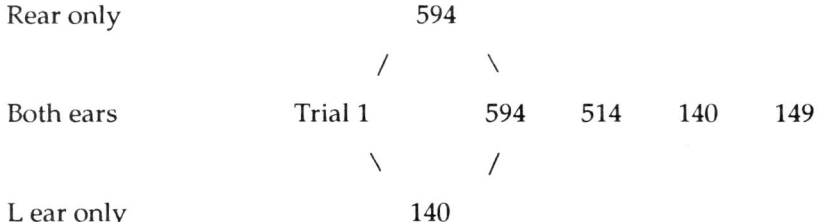

Figure 3. Diagram of what each ear hears on a given trial.

Results and Discussion Of the two false alternatives, each had two items in common with one triad and one with the other. This control prevented correct responses based on partial recognition.

The dependent variable was the number of errors made on right ear and left ear triads. The right ear had a mean error rate of 22.9%, while the left ear had an error rate of 26.9%. This was found significant with a one-tailed t-test, p<.05.

> While the results would perhaps not by themselves be very convincing evidence of a priority for the right ear, they are sufficient to confirm the difference already established... There is no indication that recognition as opposed to recall reverses the advantage of the right ear. Thus [the previous experiments] must be taken as demonstrating that the use of music rather than speech gives an advantage to the left ear. (p.360)

Running the Experiment The experiment is identical to Broadbent's original study. You will achieve best results if you can listen to the digit triads through ear phones.

Data Analysis Data analysis requires a little reorganization on your part. There are two responses required for each trial, one for the left ear and one for the right. In SuperLab value codes are associated with individual trials, so we cannot separately code the responses for the left and right ears in the data file. However, you can recode the data file with that information yourself. The first response in each trial is either event #178 or #179 and codes their left ear accuracy. The second response for a trial is either event #180 or #181, and it codes a subject's accuracy on the right ear triad for that trial. If you sort the data file by event number, you can easily organize a subject's data into trials of left and right ear responses, and then compute their accuracy across the set of trials for each ear.

Experiment 5
Studies of interference in serial verbal reactions Summaries

Stroop, J. (1935). Studies of interference in serial verbal reactions. *Journal of Experimental Psychology*, **18**, 643-662.

Introduction Stroop noticed that two functions could form an association with each other in a way that interferes with other related functions. Such inhibitory effects could be seen while reading.

> If the word "red" is printed in blue ink how will the interference of the ink-color "blue" upon reading the printed word "red" compare with the interference of the printed word "red" upon calling the name of the ink-color "blue?" The increase in time

for reacting to words caused by the presence of conflicting color stimuli is taken as the measure of the interference of color stimuli upon reading words. The increase in the time for reacting to colors caused by the presence of conflicting word stimuli is taken as the measure of the interference of word stimuli upon naming colors. (p. 646-647).

Using this observation, Stroop proposes to study the strength of interference between two associative tasks: naming and reading. He proposed that this measure may correlate with the strength of the association between related functions.

Method Seventy college undergraduates, 14 male and 56 female, were recruited as subjects for experiment one. Stimuli were four sheets with 100 color names printed on each. On two of these sheets, the color names were printed in black ink, referred to as stimulus RCNb (reading color names black). On the other two sheets the words were printed in the same order but printed in a color different from the color name, for example, the word 'red' was printed in green ink. This type of stimulus was referred to as RCNd (reading color names different). Presentation order of the sheets was counterbalanced between subjects, but always with the first and last sheets read being RCNb. There were five different color names: red, blue, green, brown, and purple.

> No word was printed in the color it named but an equal number of times in each of the other four colors; i.e., the word 'red' was printed in blue, green, brown, and purple inks; the word 'blue' was printed in red, green, brown, and purple inks; etc. (p.648).

Subjects were instructed to read each word as quickly as possible, correcting all errors before moving on.

In experiment two, 88 undergraduates (29 male, 59 female) and 12 female graduate students served as subjects.

> For this experiment the colors of the words in the RCNd test...were printed in the same order but in the form of solid squares...instead of words [referred to as the naming color, NC, test]. The RCNd test was employed also but in a very different manner from that in Experiment 1. In this experiment the colors of the print of the series of names were to be called in succession ignoring the colors named by the wording, e.g. where the word 'red' was printed in blue it was to be called 'blue' [naming color word different NCWd]. (p.649-650)

Half of the subjects were presented NC sheets first and last, with NCWd sheets in between, and half in the opposite manner. They were asked to name the colors of the items as quickly as possible, correcting all errors. Sample stimuli are shown in figure 4.

green   **green**   xxxxx

Figure 4. From left to right, stimuli in RCNd format, black ink format (from Experiment 1), and wordless format (from Experiment 2).

Results

His results from experiment one are presented in Table 1. Subjects took an average of 2.3 seconds longer to read the colored words than the black words.

Sex	No. Ss	RCNd	SD	RCNb	SD	Dif.	PEd	D/PEd
M	14	43.20	4.98	40.81	4.97	2.41	1.27	1.89
F	56	43.32	6.42	41.04	4.78	2.28	0.72	3.16
Both	70	43.30	6.15	41.00	4.84	2.30	0.63	3.64

Table 1. Mean RT for RCNd and RCNb. RCNd = "Reading color names where the color of the print and the word are different," RCNb = "Reading color names printed in black," SD = standard deviations, Dif. = differences, PEd = probable error of the difference, and D/PEd = reliability of the difference.

In experiment 2, when subjects attempted to name the color of a conflicting color-word, mean time more than doubled increasing from 63.3 for naming a color without a conflicting word to 110.3 seconds, $p<.05$.

Discussion

The difference between the mean time it took subjects to read the colored versus the black words was not statistically significant. However, a significant interference effect was found for naming the color of a conflicting color-word.

> Since the presence of the color stimuli caused no reliable increase over the normal time for reading words and the presence of word stimuli caused a considerable increase over the normal time for naming colors, the associations that have been formed between the word stimuli and the reading response are evidently more effective than those that have been formed between the color stimuli and the naming response. Since these associations are products of training, and since the difference in their strength corresponds roughly to the difference in training in reading words and naming colors, it seems reasonable to conclude that the difference in speed in

reading names of colors and in naming colors may be satisfactorily accounted for by the difference in training in the two activities. (p.659-660)

Running the Experiment Although the original experiment used 70 subjects, the "Stroop Effect" is strong enough to see for only a single subject. Experiment 3 from Stroop's original paper has been omitted.

Several adaptations have been made to the original experiment. For the purposes of computer presentation, each trial appears on a separate screen, and a microphone is required to measure reaction time as vocal onset latency. There are 120 trials in each experiment. For the Macintosh, there are three experiments. In the first experiment, the first twenty trials are color names printed in black ink, while the remaining names are printed in color in the RCNd format. Subjects are asked to read the word aloud. In Experiment 2, the first twenty stimuli are colored "xxxxx"es, removing the effect of word interference. The remaining stimuli are, again, in the RCNd format. Subjects are asked to name the color. For the Windows version, the experiment is designed to measure RT decision using the keyboard for the color of the text, comparing RCNd to control trials with colored "xxxxx"es. Experimenters should prepare colored tabs to put over five keys on the keyboard before they try to run a subject. These tabs will help subjects identify which key to press. The experiment uses the [Z] key for Blue, [X] for Green, [C] for Brown, [V] for Purple, and [B] for Red.

Data Analysis For the Macintosh version, there are four trial code values: trial, word, hue, and to say. The trial values are control or experimental. Control trials present the words in black hue. Words describes the text which is shown, e.g., the words red, blue, brown, green or purple. Hue describes the color of the text. "To say" describes what the subject was instructed to do: either to read the word (word) or say the color of text (hue). For the Windows version there is only the trial code for control or experimental trials.

Experiment 6
A feature-integration theory of attention

Treisman, A., & Gelade, G. (1980). A feature-integration theory of attention. Cognitive *Psychology,* **12**, 97-136. Reprinted by permission of Academic Press.

Introduction Treisman proposed new theory of attention, in which separate features such as color and direction of movement are perceived first, and later integrated into whole objects. This experiment explores one portion of this theory related to visual search.

> If, as we assume, simple features can be detected in parallel with no attention limits, the search for targets defined by such features (e.g., red, or vertical) should be little affected by variations in the number of distractors in the display. ...In contrast, we assume that focal attention is necessary for the detection of targets that are defined by a conjunction of properties (e.g., a vertical red line in a background of horizontal red and vertical green lines). Such targets should therefore be found only after a serial scan of varying numbers of distractors. (p.99)

Her model also suggested that given sufficient practice, such a conjunction of properties may be redefined as a single feature, thus allowing the use of the more efficient parallel search.

Method Six subjects (four male, two female) between the ages of 24 and 29 participated in the study. Displays showed 1, 5, 15, or 30 items. Eight displays in each condition contained the target (either a blue letter [T or X] or an S in the feature condition, a green T in the conjunction condition). The remaining items were distractors (brown Ts and green Xs). There were also eight displays for each condition containing only distractors. Each display was shown for one second. Subjects were to press one key if they detected the target, another if they did not. They were instructed to respond as quickly as possible without making any errors. Feedback was given on reaction time and accuracy.

All subjects participated in three blocks of 128 trials in each condition. Two volunteered to continue for four more such blocks, and two others volunteered for ten. All blocks randomized presentation of different sized displays.

Results and Discussion Results from Figure 5 show that search times increased linearly with display size in the conjunction condition, suggesting that the search process was conducted serially, one item at a time, at a rate of about 60 ms per item. The results for the feature condition, however, are more consistent with a parallel search. Search times were only marginally affected by the number of distractors.

These results suggest that subjects use serial search when the target involves more than one feature, but can scan in parallel many objects when searching for a target with a single feature. The secondary hypothesis, concerning the switch from serial to parallel with practice, was not supported. Subjects who continued for extra blocks showed no significant change in performance pattern for conjunction targets.

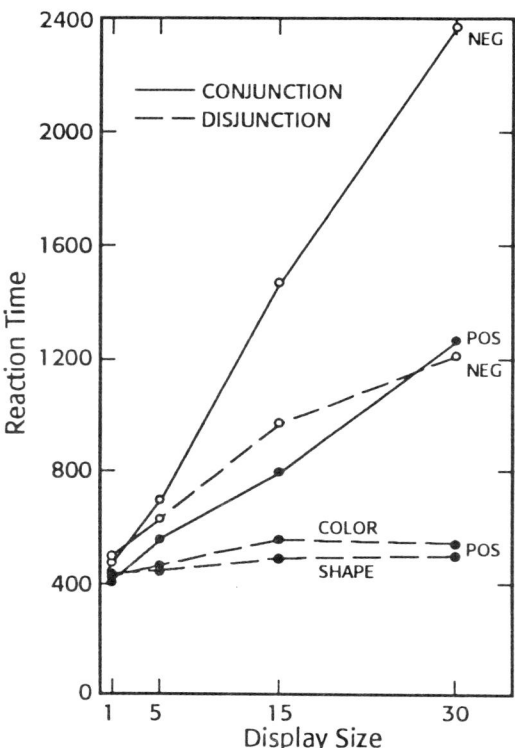

Figure 5. Search for colored shapes: search times for the experiment.

Running the Experiment Experiment 1 of their study is presented with 64 conjunction and 64 feature targets.

Data Analysis There are three trial variables: condition, response, and display size. Condition defines the target as conjunc(tion) or feature. Resp(onse) defines if the target was present (pos) or absent (neg). Disp(lay) size defines the number of items in the display (1, 5, 15, or 30).

Experiment 7
Temporal integration and segregation of brief visual stimuli : patterns of correlation in time

---

Dilollo, V., Hogben, J., & Dixon, P. (1994). Temporal integration and segregation of brief visual stimuli: patterns of correlation in time. *Perception and Psychophysics*, **55**, 373-386. Reprinted by permission of the Psychonomic Society, Inc.

Introduction   *Visible persistence* refers to the fact that visual stimuli remain visible for a brief time after the display has been turned off. As the duration of the original stimulus is decreased, the duration of persistence is increased. Various explanations have been made for this "inverse duration effect."

> According to [the] processing hypothesis, visible persistence corresponds to a period of neural activity (which we refer to as the *visual response*) that starts at stimulus onset and lasts for a fixed period, irrespective of stimulus duration. (p. 373)

When the stimulus is short, the duration of persistence outlasts the physical display, but the longer the stimulus lasts, the more it overlaps with the persistence response of the visual nervous system, thus shortening persistence. For long durations, persistence and the physical exposure completely overlap, and persistence disappears.

When two stimuli are presented in rapid succession they are *temporally integrated* and seen as a single visual event. Under the processing hypothesis, integration occurs when the visible persistence of the first stimulus overlaps the onset of the second. The only factor affecting whether or not it occurs is the Stimulus Onset Asynchrony (SOA: the time between the onset of the first stimulus and the onset of the second).

A different prediction is made by the *temporal correlation model*. According to this theory, the correlation between two visual responses is calculated neurally.

> According to the processing hypothesis, stimulus duration and ISI are equivalent; increasing the duration of one while decreasing the other by the same amount should have no effect on temporal integration. By contrast, according to the correlational model, temporal integration should be affected more by a change in ISI than by a corresponding change in stimulus duration. (p. 375)

This study was designed to test the predictions of the processing and temporal integration models.

Methods   Subjects were two of the authors and a colleague, all of whom had normal or corrected-to-normal vision. The task involved viewing two stimuli in rapid succession. Each showed twelve dots. When viewed together, they showed 24 out of 25 possible dots on a five by five grid. The display subtended a viewing angle of eight degrees and was presented in a dimly lit room. Subjects were to identify the missing dot, possible only if temporal integration took place.

There were seven possible durations of the initial stimulus (20, 40, 60, 80, 100, 120, and 140 msec) and eight possible ISIs (all of the above as well as a 0 ISI condition), resulting in 56 possible conditions. The second stimulus always appeared for 10 msec. Each subject ran in 35 sessions of 160 trials each. Sessions were blocked by initial stimulus duration.

Results and Discussion

As can be seen in Figure 6, the results were not determined by SOA alone.

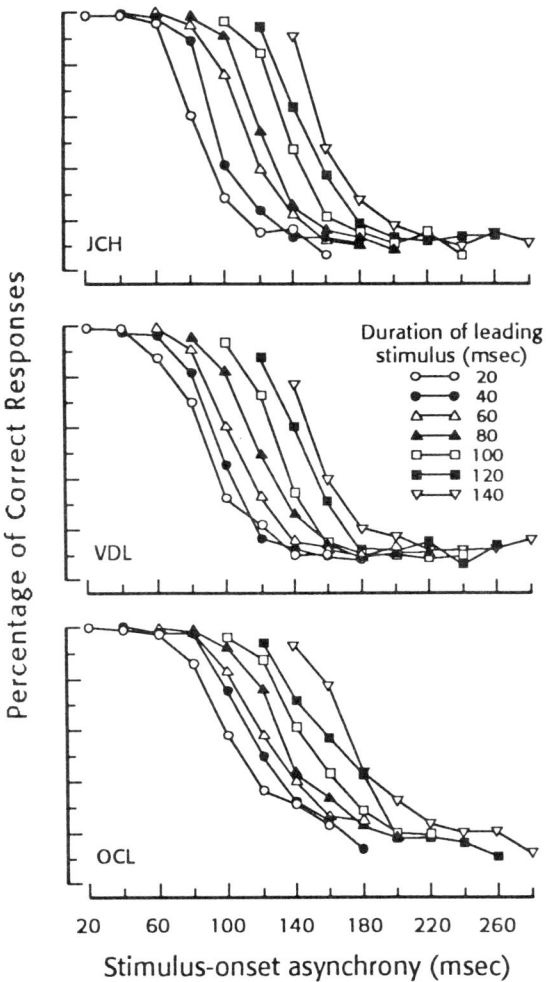

Figure 6. Performance as a function of SOA, shown separately for each observer. Separate curves are plotted for each duration of the leading display.

> Had SOA been the sole determinant, there would have been a single level of performance associated with each SOA, or, equivalently, a single performance curve for each observer. Instead, any given level of SOA in Figure [6] exhibits a range of performance levels, depending on the combination of exposure duration and ISI. (p.375-76)

These results do not support the processing hypothesis, but do provide evidence for a temporal correlation theory. The authors elaborate the theory with a mathematical model based on their findings.

Running the Experiment

Dilollo et. al.'s first experiment is presented here with some modification. Only four durations of the first image and four ISIs for a total of 16 conditions are included. Each condition is used six times for a total of 96 trials. All room lights must be off before running this experiment. There is a practice and experiment version. There are 48 practice trials. Do them all; it's a hard task.

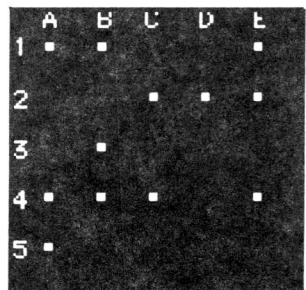 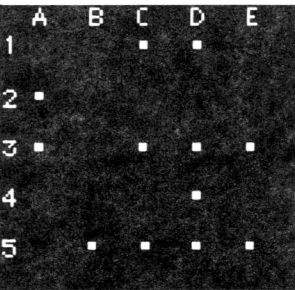

Figure 7. Two images which, when integrated, result in a 5x5 matrix with dot B2 missing.

Data Analysis

Trials are coded for four variables: duration, ISI, letter and number. Duration defines the exposure of the leading stimulus at 20, 60, 100 and 140 ms. ISI defines the interval between the two stimuli at 0, 40, 80 and 120 ms. Letter and number identifies the position of the missing dot.

Memory

Experiment 8
Depth of processing and the retention of words

Craik, F. & Tulving, E. (1975). Depth of processing and the retention of words in episodic memory. *Journal of Experimental Psychology: General*, **104**, 268-294. Copyright (1975) by the American Psychological Association. Reprinted with permission.

Introduction

The experiment reported here is one of several designed to explore the authors' Depth of Processing theory of memory.

> The basic notions are that the episodic memory trace may be thought of as a rather automatic by-product of operations carried out by the cognitive system and that the durability of

The Experiments

> the trace is a positive function of "depth" of processing, where
> depth refers to greater degrees of semantic involvement. (p.268)

According to this theory, words processed more deeply should have stronger, more durable traces--and thus be easier to recall.

Method Twenty college students served as subjects. Thirty-six common, two-syllable nouns of 5-7 letters length were presented for 200 ms each. Before each word was presented subjects were asked a question about it, which they had to answer as quickly as possible without making errors after the word appeared. Five types of questions were used. In ordering of increasing level of processing required, they were: (1) "Is there a word present?" (The four negative trials for this were blank screens, making a total of 40 trials.) (2) "Is the word in capital letters?" (3) "Does the word rhyme with _____?" (4) "Is the word in the category _____?" (5) "Would the word fit in the sentence _____?" There were four positive and four negative instances of each question type. Assignment of words to each of the ten possible combinations of question and answer was rotated across subjects. When the list presentation was complete, subjects were given a brief rest. They were then given a sheet with the 40 words they had seen plus 40 similar distractors, and asked to circle the words they had seen. There was no time limit for the recall task.

Results and Discussion Questions which were classified as requiring deeper levels of processing were confirmed as having longer response times by ANOVA (F = 35.4, p<.001).

| | Level of Processing | | | | |
Response Type	1	2	3	4	5
	Response Latency (msec)				
Yes	591	614	689	711	746
No	590	625	678	716	832
	Proportion Recognized				
Yes	22	18	78	93	96
No		14	36	63	83

Table 2. Initial Decision Latency and Recognition Performance for Words as a Function of Initial Task.

Recognition performance increased from 22% for words processed at the lowest level to 96% for Level 5 words. This effect was found significant by ANOVA (F = 52.8, p<.001). In addition, "Yes" response words were significantly better recognized than "no" words (F = 40.2, p<.001).

These results support their theory: greater depth of processing does indeed appear to lead to greater retention.

Running the Experiment   There are six counter-balanced versions of their first experiment using the stimuli reported in their appendix. Each student should be assigned to one. In this version subjects complete 60 trials, and we have included on three of their five level of processing conditions: letter case, word rhyme, and word category. Recall is made item by item.

Data Analysis   Trials are codes by case, depth, and pos/neg. Case defines whether the text was presented in upper or lower case. Depth defines the level of processing: type (as in upper/lower type), phon (phonics for examining whether words rhymed) and meaning (for semantic categorization). Pos/neg defined if the answer should be yes or no.

Experiment 9
Mental processes revealed by reaction time experiments

Sternberg, S. (1966). High-speed scanning in human memory. Sternberg, S. (1966).Sternberg, S. (1966). High-speed scanning in human memory. *Science, 66,* 652-654. Reprinted by permission of the author, S. Sternberg.

Introduction   Mental functions are often conceived as a series of stages through which stimuli are processed. In a simple reaction time (RT) task, the RT is the sum of the time it takes all functions to complete their operations. Sternberg proposed to decompose the RT into its different processing stages, thereby revealing the sequence and processing time of different mental functions.

The results from experiment one, a memory recall task, are described here. In this study, Sternberg explored the functions of recognition and memory recall using an experimental task in which subjects compared a target stimulus to a given stimulus set, and determined whether or not it was a member of that set. He proposed that theoretically this task could be accomplished by two types of a serial searches.

> Let *serial search* (or *scanning*) be a process in which each of a set of items is compared one at a time, and no more than once, to a target item. ...The purpose of the search is to determine whether an agreement (or *match*) exists between the test item and any of the items in the memorized set. Two types of serial search that might serve this purpose need to be considered. In *self-terminating serial search*, the test stimulus is compared successively to one item in memory after another, either until a match occurs (leading to a positive response), or until all comparisons have been completed without a match (leading to

a negative response). In *exhaustive serial search*, the test stimulus is compared successively to *all* the memorized items. Only then is a response made -- positive if a match has occurred, and negative otherwise. (p.426-427)

Sternberg proposed that exhaustive search could be distinguished from self-terminating searches by the way in which a target stimulus was positively or negatively recalled.

In an exhaustive search the test stimulus is compared to all items in memory before each positive response as well as before a negative response. Hence, the rate at which RT increases with list length--the slope of the RT-function--is the same for positive and negative responses. In contrast, a self-terminating search stops in the middle of the list, on the average, before positive responses, but continues through the entire list before negatives. The result is that as list length is increased, the latency of positive responses increases at half the rate of the increase for negatives. (p.427-428)

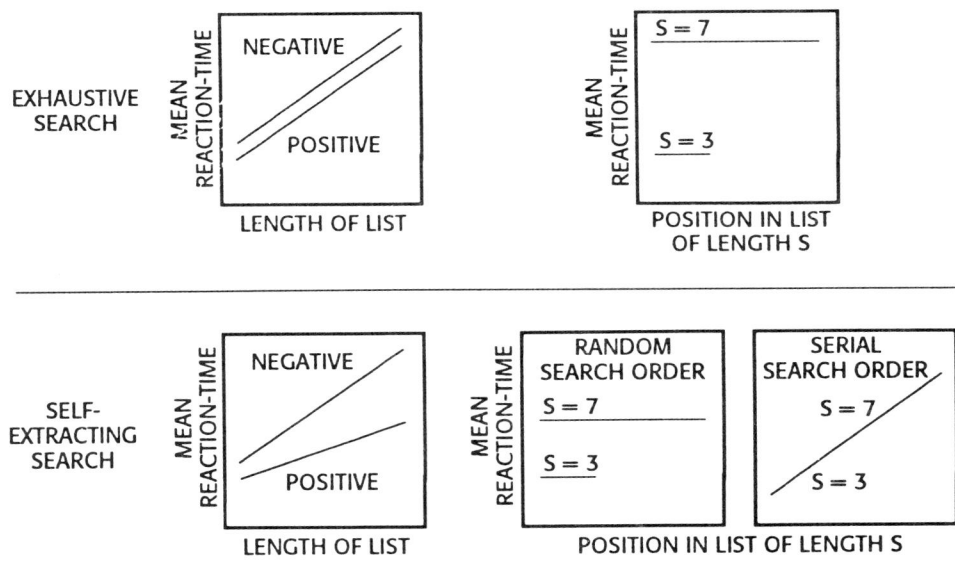

Figure 8. Some properties of exhaustive (top) and self-terminating (bottom) serial searches. Left: Theoretical RT-functions (mean latencies of positive and negative responses as functions of length of list). Right: Theoretical serial-position functions (mean latency of positive responses as a function of serial position of test item in a list of given length).

Method Subjects were given a set of digits to memorize (the *positive set*) followed by a probe digit. Subjects determined whether the probe is a member of this set. Sets of digits varied in size. Which method was used would change the slope as the set size increases.

Eight subjects were presented with sets of one to six different digits on each trial at a rate of 1.2 seconds per digit. Two seconds after the last digit in the set, subjects received a warning signal followed by the presentation of a probe digit. They were asked to determine as quickly as possible whether the probe had been in the set.

Results and Discussion Figure 9 shows the results from experiment one. The slope of the line was linear, averaging 38 ms per memory item and had a zero intercept at 400 ms. At this rate, subjects appeared to be able to scan memory at a very rapid rate of about 25-30 digits per second. Positive and negative responses showed similar slopes. These results are consistent with the diagram in the upper left-hand corner of Figure 8, suggesting that subject used an exhaustive search when accessing short-term memory.

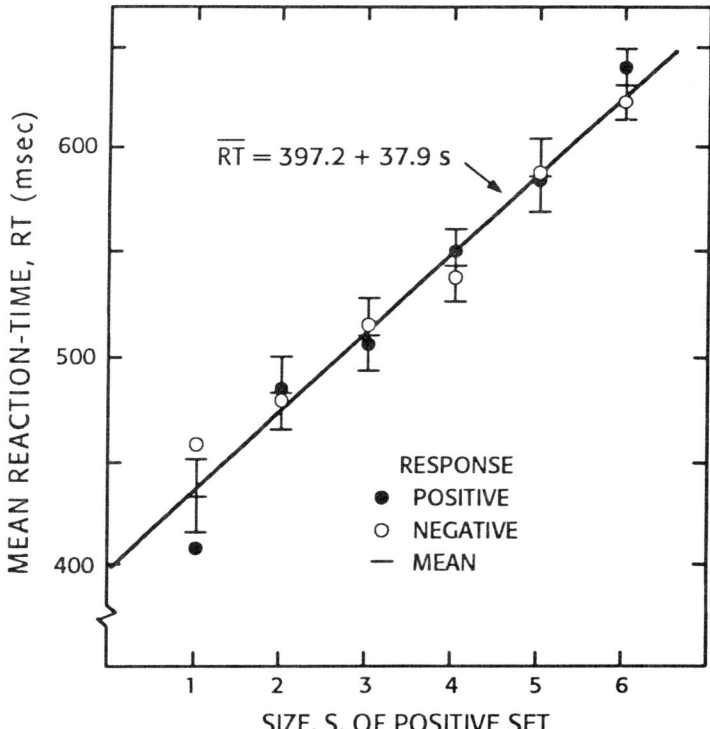

Figure 9. Results of Experiment 1: Item-recognition with varied-set procedure. Mean latencies of correct positive and negative responses, and their average, as functions of positive set size.

Running the Experiment This experiment is unchanged from the original.

Data Analysis Trials have two code values: set size (1, 2, 3, 4, 5, 6) and target (in set or foil).

Experiment 10
Knowledge structures in the organization and retrieval of autobiographical memories

Reiser, B. J., Black, J. B., and Abelson, R. P. (1985). Knowledge structures in the organization and retrieval of autobiographical memories. *Cognitive Psychology*, **17**, 89-137.

Introduction Reiser, Black, and Abelson propose that autobiographical events are organized in memory by the knowledge structures that guided comprehension and planning during the experience. Two such structural types are activities (sequences of actions performed to achieve a goal) and general actions (situation-free components common to several activities). Activities are broader events like going to a restaurant or getting a haircut. General actions are small things that often can be part of many activities, such as paying the bill (something one does at both a restaurant and the barber) or ordering a drink. Activities are thought to be more important to facilitate memorization. Reiser et. al. suggest an almost hierarchical organization of memory where general actions are subordinately categorized to activities.

> ...if activities are the principal categories for individual experiences, presentation of an activity before a general action should lead to faster retrieval of an experience matching both cues. When the action is presented first, the information available for memory search is less useful until a contextualizing activity can be found to augment it, so retrieval should be slower for these cases. (p.103)

Methods Data was collected from 32 undergraduate students ages 17 to 21. Subjects received 4 practice trials and 20 experimental trials. Each trial started when the subject pressed a key. A phrase which was an action or activity appeared on the screen for 5 seconds before the second phrase appeared below it (an action if the first phrase was an activity, or vice versa). Subjects were instructed to press the 'Yes' key as soon as they had a specific experience in mind which fit these phrases, or the 'No' key as soon as they decided that they could not recall any such experience.

Stimuli were constructed so that there were twenty separate activities and twenty general actions. Each general action could be applied to two different activities, and half the actions were regular actions while half were failure actions (i.e. 'didn't get what you wanted' or 'couldn't find a seat').

Results and Discussion   After removing outliers and eliminating questionable data, the results fit extremely well with their original hypothesis. Subjects recalled an autobiographical experience two seconds faster when cued by an activity rather than a general action (min F'(1,45) = 12.12, p <.01).

This experiment is particularly important to psychologists because it provides a framework for the empirical study of autobiographical memory. Before this study, autobiographical research was avoided because there was no way to compare personal memories from one person to another.

Running the Experiment   There are four counterbalanced versions of their first experiment; students should be assigned to only one. For the second part of the experiment you will also need a pen and a printout of the response sheet.

Data Analysis   Each trial has two variables: first phrase and action type. First phrase defines whether the first phrase was an activity or general action. Phrases also were defined by their action type: either regular or failures. RT for each trial type can be tabulated by computer, although you will have to check subject written responses as well to confirm compliance with instructions or to eliminate memories that don't meet criteria. Be sure to sort the data by response keys to eliminate trials where the subject couldn't remember an event (e.g., all trials with a [Z] key response.)

Perceptual Representation

Experiment 11
Spontaneous imagery scanning in Mental extrapolation

Finke, R. & Pinker, S. (1982). Spontaneous imagery scanning in mental extrapolation. *Journal of Experimental Psychology: Learning, Memory and Cognition*, 8, 142-147.

Introduction   Previous experiments have shown that as the distance between features in a mental image increases, so does the response time required for scanning those features. Critics have argued that these results may be due to aspects of the task other than mental imagery, such as the subject's knowledge of the laws governing physical motion. To address this concern Finke and Pinker used a paradigm that required mental image scanning. Subjects viewed a display of dots for a short period of time. Then the display was removed and an arrow was shown which may or may not point to one of the dot locations. To complete this task successfully, subjects would have to work from a mental image of the display, extrapolating along the line of the arrow to determine if a dot was in that path.

Method All 12 subjects had normal or corrected-to-normal vision. At the beginning of each trial, subjects freely inspected a dot pattern that was presented for 5 sec, with instructions to remember the positions of the dots. A blank screen was then presented for 1 sec, followed by a field that contained a single black which was presented for 4 sec. The subjects' task was to respond 'yes' if the arrow on a particular trial was pointing to any of the dots that they had just observed, and to respond 'no' if the arrow was not. They were instructed to do so as quickly and as accurately as possible. They were informed that this judgment task would not be difficult, because the arrows would either be pointing directly at a dot or clearly miss all of the dots. The same four patterns were shown on eight consecutive trials, so that the effects of pattern familiarity could be examined separately from other effects. Subjects were given feedback regarding their accuracy.

The distance between the arrow and the dot was varied, being either 4, 6, 8, 10 or 12 cm. Each distance occurred only once for each pattern. The locations and orientations of arrows for each type of response were equally distributed across the field.

Results and Discussion Finke and Pinker found that errors were relatively infrequent, occurring on 4.6% of the trials. However, reaction time did increase with the distance between arrow and dot ($F_{4,40}$) = 9.79, $p<.001$, and there was a very strong correlation between reaction time and distance ($r = .94$). The apparent rate of scanning of 19.5 msec/cm was consistent with the previous findings of other researchers.

Six of the twelve subjects reported that they had found it necessary to scan mental images in order to make their judgments. Five of the remaining six subjects reported that they had remembered using images of the patterns in some way. This suggests that mental image scanning was used by all but one of the subjects to complete the task.

This experiment confirmed previous studies that mental images can be scanned with a duration that increases linearly with increasing distance between the source and destination of scanning. However, unlike the previous experiments, subjects did not use mental images because they were instructed to do so, but because they found it to be the most efficient way to perform the required task.

Running the Experiment This original experiment is presented unchanged.

Data Analysis Trials code two variables: pattern and distance. Pattern defines the dot pattern presented (I, II, III, or IV). Distance defines the viewing distance between the arrow and dot (4, 6, 8, 10, or 12 cms or none when the arrow did not point to a dot).

> Experiment 12
> The effect of landmark features on mental rotation times

Hochberg, J. and Gellman, L. (1977). The effect of landmark features on mental rotation times. *Memory and Cognition*, **5**, 23-26. Reprinted by permission of Psychonomic Society, Inc.

Introduction Shepard and his colleagues (1971, 1973) proposed a method to measure one aspect of visual imagery - the "mental rotation" of objects. In their task, a subject examined two shapes to determine if they are the same or different, making this judgment by mentally rotating one of shapes. They proposed that the mental process is analogous to physical rotation and that it takes place at a set rate. Hochberg and Gellman write:

> As the angle between orientations of two shapes is increased, subjects who have been trained in "mental rotation" take longer to decide that the shapes are the same and not mirror images of each other. Because Shepard and his colleagues have found that the time/angle function is always monotonic and often remarkably linear for a variety of tasks and circumstances, they argue that the task is performed by means of an underlying "analog" process, proceeding at a rate of approximately 60 deg/sec. (p.23)

Shephard had varied the complexity of the shapes to be rotated, but the features were not matched for orientation and location. Hochberg and Gellman proposed that *landmarks* or "cues to location and orientation that are unique and visible from a distance" may be a critical factor in mental rotation performance.

> To be useful in the mental rotation task, a landmark feature must either provide direct information about orientation, even when it falls in peripheral vision, or must indicate where the subject will find such information by directing his fovea to the landmark's vicinity. (p.23)

This experiment was designed to vary stimulus complexity according to the landmark model.

Method Five stimuli were designed of with varying levels of landmark salience.

> In Shape E, the cue to orientation is unique and peripherally visible. In...C and D, redundant and irrelevant features were added ...so that they would mask each other when viewed peripherally. ...In the two remaining shapes, A and B, the sets

of features or details are sufficiently far from each other that the subject would not be expected to resolve the details and their spatial order properly and, therefore, would not know on the basis of peripheral information alone whether the two examples were the same, nor where to look in order to compare their corresponding parts. (p.23-24)

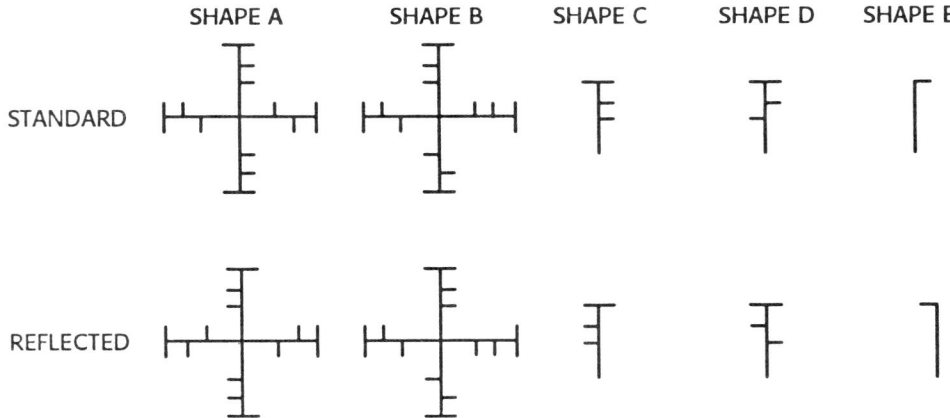

Figure 10. Stimuli used for mental rotation.

Three right-handed undergraduates without previous mental rotation experience served as subjects. The experiment consisted of 300 trials. Each trial contained either two figures of the same shape, or a shape and its mirror image.

> The left shape was rotated to some multiple of 20 degrees, the right shape was set at 0, 40, 80, 120, or 160 degrees clockwise. ...In all, there were six "same" and six "different" trials for each of the five levels of angular difference in orientation, for each of the five stimulus shapes. (p.24)

Figure 11. Sample trial stimuli. On the left, a "different" trial for Shape A, requiring 60 degrees of rotation. On the right, a "same" trial for Shape D, also requiring 60 degrees of rotation.

Subjects were instructed in the mental rotation method, and asked always to rotate the right-hand shape clockwise. They were asked to press the right-hand switch for "same" trials, and the left-hand switch for "different" trials. Example trial stimuli are presented in Figure 11.

Results and Discussion Mean reaction time for "same" judgments are shown in Figure 12. "Different" judgment times varied widely and were not reported in the original article.

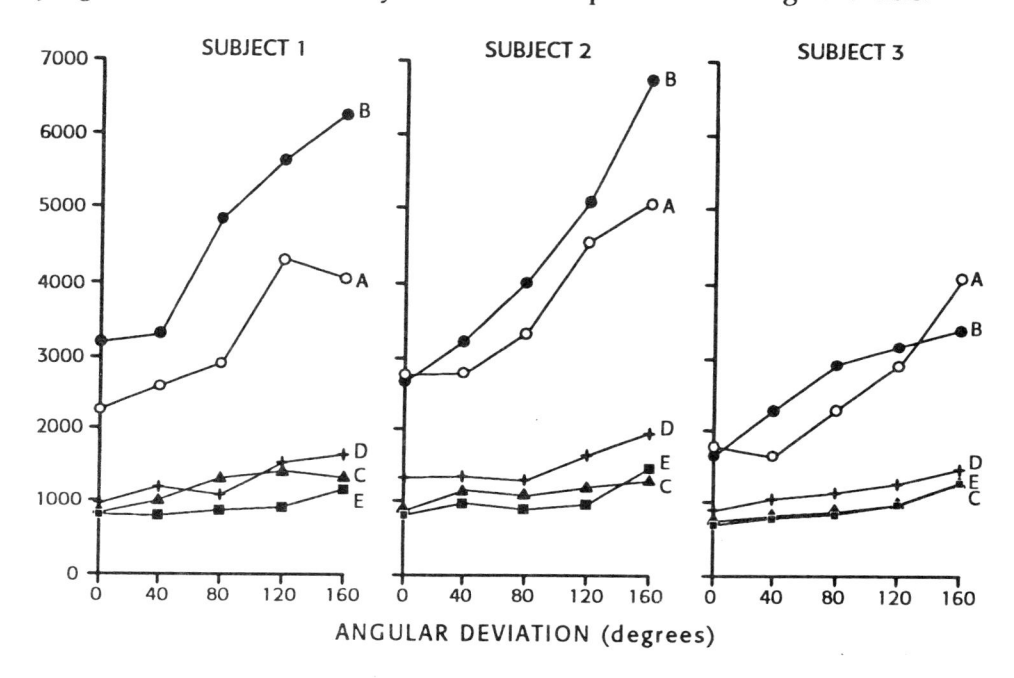

Figure 12. Mean reaction times for "same judgments as a function of angular difference in orientation, for each shape and for each subject.

ANOVAs showed significant effects of shape on the slope (p<.001) and the intercept (p<.001). All subjects had higher slopes and intercepts for Shapes A and B compared to C, D, and E. As predicted, shapes with the salient landmarks (C, D, E) had lower slopes and intercepts than those which were more difficult to distinguish (A, B). These results suggested that more feature comparisons were required to distinguish shapes A and B, suggesting that the mental rotation task "task reflects the processes by which perceived forms are built up over successive glances."

Running the Experiment The number of experiment trials was cut to 150 providing three "same" and three "different" trials for each of the five levels of angular difference in orientation, for each of the five stimulus shapes.

Data Analysis Data analysis is a little tricky here. There are three trial code values: angle difference, same/diff and shape. The angle codes the degree of clockwise rotation needed for the left image to be superimposed on the right image. There are 18 different trial angles at 20 degree increments, but the SuperLab code editor limits the number of values to 10, so a second code (angle dif2) has been specified to code angle values between 200 and 340 degrees. In the data file there will be a single angle code for each trial but the code values are distributed across two columns, depending on the angle. One column will be blank but the other will have the correct value. Data from both columns need to be combined into a single column before proceeding with further analyses. The same/different code describes the match between the two images. The shape defines one of the five types of shapes in the experiment (A-E).

References Cited

Cooper, L. A., & Shepard, R. N. (1973). Chronometric studies of the rotation of mental images. In W. G. Chase (Ed.), *Visual information processing*. New York: Academic Press.

Shepard, R. N., & Metzer, J. (1971). Mental rotation of three dimensional objects. *Science*, **171**, 701-703.

Experiment 13
The Rate of mental rotation of images: A test of a holistic analogue hypothesis

Pylyshyn, Z. (1979). The Rate of mental rotation of images: A test of a holistic analogue hypothesis. *Memory and Cognition*, **7**, 19-28. Reprinted by permission of the Psychonomic Society, Inc.

Introduction

Many studies have found evidence that the mind organizes information into propositional representations. A proposition, in this sense, is the simplest unit of thought which could be true or false. For example, *John loves Mary* is a proposition, but *John* or *loves* are incomplete thoughts.

Some researchers have argued that visual imagery cannot be reduced to a propositional framework and operates using a different analogue structure in which the visual display is mentally reconstructed and manipulated in the mind. For example, if you are asked how many pennies make a dime, you don't need to imagine what a dime looks like to answer "ten." However, you probably will picture a dime in your mind if you are asked to describe in detail what the two sides of a dime actually look like.

Pylyshyn has argued that many of the phenomena that support analogue processing show "cognitive penetration"; that is, a subject's beliefs can influence their performance on these analogue tasks, suggesting that the phenomena under study can be affected by propositional cognitive operations as well. In this study he shows that mental rotation of objects, a phenomena which some believed was a pure analogue operation, can be affected by subjects' judgments.

Method There were 16 subjects. In the usual mental rotation paradigm, subjects are shown two figures and asked to rotate the second in order to determine whether it is the same as the first, or a mirror image. In this experiment, they were asked whether the second was a subfigure of the first. The stimuli and their possible subfigure probes are shown in Figure 13. From top to bottom figures become increasingly more complex (with more possible subfigures), and from left to right subfigures become increasingly less obvious. All probes contain the baseline of the figure. "False" probes were the mirror images of those shown.

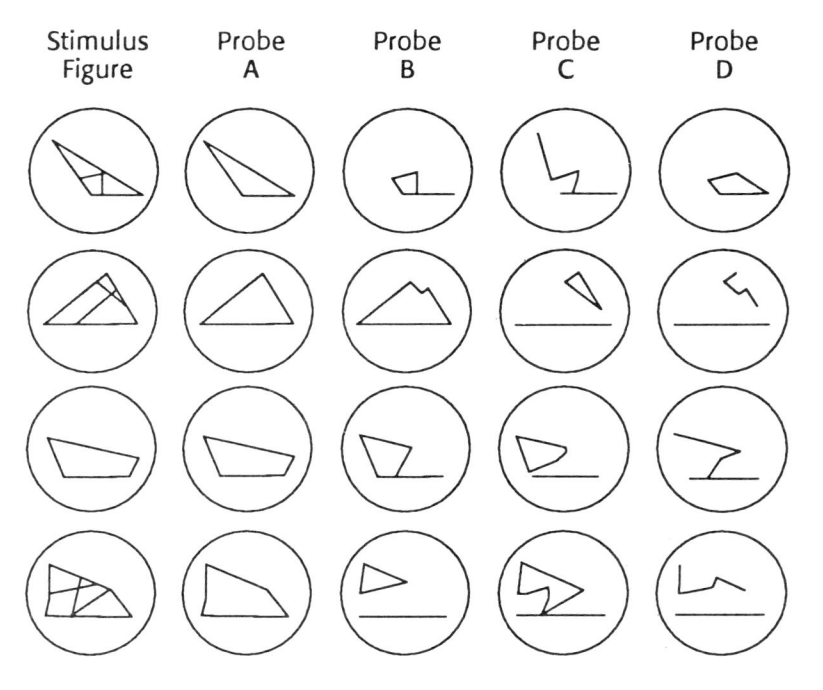

Figure 13. Stimulus figures and "true" probes used in the experiment. Distractor trials used either mirror images of the probes shown or the above probes paired with mirror image stimuli. Figures are numbered top down (1-4).

There was one practice session and four experimental sessions of 128 trials each. Each session was divided into four 32-trial blocks with breaks in between. Subjects were instructed mentally to rotate the left figure until it matched the baseline of the right figure or probe and then decide if the probe was a subfigure of the left figure.

Results and Discussion Results were analyzed from true pairs only. As can be seen in Figure 14, reaction time increases linearly as the angle through which the probe must be rotated increases (F = 96, p<.001). However, it does so differentially for figures of different complexity (F = 5.6, p<.005).

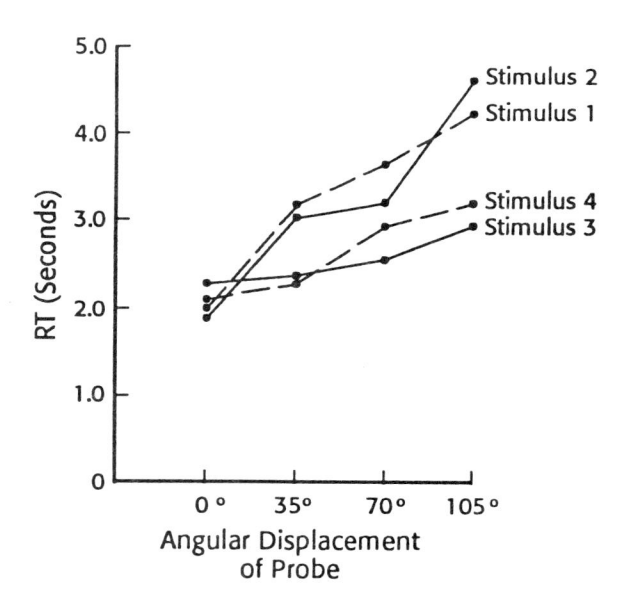

Figure 14. Mean reaction time functions for the four different stimulus figures (plus their mirror images) using the outline probes (Probe A) only.

All but Stimulus 2 showed a significant effect of probe on reaction time (Stimulus 1: F = 6.95, p<.005; Stimulus 3: F = 3.35, p<.03; Stimulus 4: F = 3.35, p<.03). All but Stimulus 1 showed a significant effect of practice on the linear trend (Stimulus 2: F = 9.02, p<.01; Stimulus 3: F = 7.38, p<.02; Stimulus 4: F = 9.51, p<.01).

The author states that

> The apparent "rate of mental rotation" is a function of (1) practice, (2) intrinsic properties of the stimulus, and (3) the nature of the comparison task carried out on the rotated image. (p.26)

He concludes that the factors affecting mental rotation are far too numerous and complex to be labeled only as "analogue."

Running the Experiment The first experiment from Pylyshyn's study is replicated. It contains 135 trials: 64 true, 64 mirror, and 7 foils.

Data Analysis Four variables are used to define trials: subfigure, rotation, figure, and probe. Subfigures are defined as true, mirror, or foil. Rotation define the degree of rotation needed to match figure baselines: 0, 35, 70, or 105 degrees. Figure defines the complexity of the stimulus figure increasing from 1 (simple), through 2, 3, and 4 (most complex). The probe variable defines the difficulty of detecting the subfigure in the probe, increasing from A (easy), through B, C, D (hard), and foil (not a subfigure).

> *Experiment 14*
> *Forest before trees: The precedence of global features in visual perception*

Navon, D. (1977). Forest before trees: The precedence of global features in visual perception. *Cognitive Psychology*, **9**, 353-383. Reprinted by permission from Academic Press.

Introduction

In this study Navon introduced a new paradigm to examine how the visual system processes information. He posed the problem this way:

> Do we perceive a visual scene feature-by-feature? Or is the process instantaneous and simultaneous as some Gestalt psychologists believed? Or is it somewhere in between? The Gestaltists' view of the perceptual system as a perfectly elastic device that can swallow and digest all visual information at once, no matter how rich it is, is probably too naive. There is ample evidence that people extract from a picture more and more as they keep looking at it. But does this mean that interpreting the picture is done by integrating information collected in a piecemeal fashion? Is the perceptual whole literally constructed out of the percepts of its elements? (p. 353)

Navon hypothesized that visual perception is organized over time with the global shape of a visual scene processed first, followed by the analysis of the fine-grained visual details. Each scene is "in a process of being focused or zoomed in on, where at first it is relatively indistinct and then it gets clearer and sharper." (p.354)

Method

Navon designed stimuli with both global and local properties. These were block letters (H, and S) composed of smaller block letters (see Figure 15).

```
S          S
S          S
S          S
S          S
SSSSSSSSSSS
S          S
S          S
S          S
S          S
```

Figure 15. An H at the global level, made up of Ss at the local level.

Fourteen undergraduate subjects with normal or corrected to normal vision were recruited. Each subject was run in two conditions. In the global-directed condition, subjects were asked to indicate whether the large letter was an H or an S. In the local-directed condition they made the same choice for the smaller letters. Subjects were asked to respond quickly while making as few errors as possible. Trials began with a 50 msec warning beep and the presentation of center fixation point. Stimuli then were presented for 40 ms, appearing randomly in each of the four quadrants of the presentation field. The stimuli were immediately followed by a dot mask. There were 144 trials in each condition.

Results and Discussion

Figure 16 presents the mean correct response latencies under the different experimental conditions. The main effects of attention $F(1,12) = 855.85$, $p<.001$ and consistency $F(2,24) = 72.48$, $p<.001$ were significant. There also was a significant interaction between these factors, $F(2,24) = 16.59$, $p<.001$.

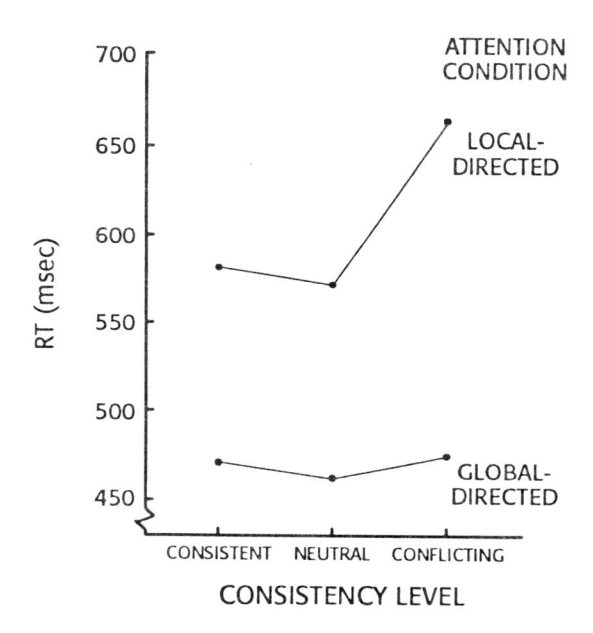

Figure 16. Mean RT for correct responses shown for consistency level and attentional conditions.

Navon concluded:

> The results of this experiment indicate that the global pattern is responded to faster than the elements. Moreover, whereas people can voluntarily attend to the global pattern without being affected by the local features, they are not able to process the local features without being aware of the whole. ...The finding that attention cannot be efficiently diverted from the whole may be interpreted as support to the notion that global

processing is a necessary stage of perception prior to more fine-grained analysis. (p. 371)

Running the Experiment Only the third of Navon's four experiments is presented here. The number of trials per condition were reduced to 36. With 40 ms presentations Navon's subjects achieved 96.7% accuracy, and therefore he analyzed the response latency data. We, however, have been unable to achieve anywhere near that level of accuracy with 40 ms durations, and recommend you use a longer duration. The duration value can be set in the ISI stimuli/event for all trials in the experiment. It is currently set to 100 ms. This is a reasonable duration for global judgments but may still be too short to detect the local letters with a high degree of accurately. In such a case you may want to analyze both accuracy and latency data.

Data Analysis Trials have three codes: global, local and block. The global and local codes define the letter shape at the global and local level (H, S or O). The block code defines the judgment subjects were asked to make: the global or local letter shape.

Experiment 15
Proofreading Errors on the Word The *: New Evidence on Reading Units*

Healy, A. (1980). Proofreading Errors on the Word *The* : New Evidence on Reading Units. *Journal of Experimental Psychology: Human Perception & Performance*, 6, 45-57. Copyright (1980) by American Psychological Association. Reprinted with permission.

Introduction Words can be processed at several different levels. They can read as a phrase, a word, or letter-by-letter, depending upon the task demands placed on the reader. In letter-detection tasks, where subjects are supposed to identify all instances of a particular letter in a prose passage, they are particularly likely to make errors on the word *the*. Healy proposed a unitization hypothesis to account for the prevalence of this mistake. Completion of processing at a higher level is thought to halt processing at lower levels, so if word-level processing is finished, there is no need to continue processing individual letters. Since *the* is the most common word in English, it is rapidly processed at the word level. For a letter detection task, this means that more errors are made on detection of individual t s in *the* because letter-level processing is rarely completed. However, accuracy could change with a different task.

The present experiment uses a proofreading task, in which subjects must detect misspelled words in a prose passage. These words are misspelled by transposing two adjacent letters; i.e., elbow becomes elobw. This change should disturb letter level processing very little, since no letters have been

The Experiments

replaced, but should greatly disturb word-level processing since it forms a non-word. In a proofreading task, Healy's model predicts a higher degree of accuracy between *the* and other words. Because *the* is a very short word, transpositions will cause greater differences between the original and misspelling. Therefore, detecting such errors on the should be relatively easy.

Method

Ninety-six undergraduate students participated as subjects. Subjects were given a 321-word prose passage taken from Eliot Aronson's The Social Animal. Forty transposition misspellings were distributed through the paragraph, 11 of which were on the word *the* (six *teh*, five *hte*.). Subjects were asked to read the passage at normal speed, circling misspellings as they came to them. They were told not to slow down in order to catch misspellings, nor to go back and correct errors they later realized they had made.

Results and Discussion

The results are shown in Table 3. The figure in the first column is calculated by 100 - (errors detected/40). The second column calculation is based on 100 - (the errors detected/11). The final column is the percentage of errors made which were on *the*, and not some other word. By chance alone this figure would be 27.5% (11/40). The actual figure is significantly below chance level, $t(92)=21.5$, $p<.001$.

Error %	p (error)	p(error on *the*)	p(error on *the*/error)
M	11.6	3.3	6.2
SEm	.8	.7	1.4

Table 3. Means and Standard Errors of Means for Percentages of Transposition-Proofreading Errors.

As further support for the hypothesis, the author tested whether word length was a predictor of error percentage for other misspelled words. Subjects made significantly more errors on 5-10 letter words than on shorter ones ($F=81.4$, $p<.001$).

These results suggests that even though common words, such as *the*, may normally be read as a whole word, they can also be read letter-by-letter when the word is misspelled.

Running the Experiment

Healy's experiment was a paper and pen task. Her original passage from experiment one of her paper is presented here by computer, one line at a time for a total of 34 lines. A few of the typographical errors found in her original passage had to be moved to other words with the same number of letters to allow a single line of text to only contain errors on the word *the*. In this way each line of text is a proofreading trial, allowing us to compare error detection accuracy on *the* to other words.

The subject's task is to proof each line of text. Each time an error is found, the space bar should be pressed. When the line has been read through, the [Z] key should be pressed.

Data Analysis Data analysis requires a bit of manipulation of the data file to compute a subject's proofreading percentage. The data file will have 34 trials. Each trial could have multiple responses. The last response will have an error code of "SC" and a response of "Z". Every time an error was found, the subject pressed the "space bar." These responses will appear for each trial with "E" error codes and the corresponding reaction time.

Two trial codes are used: word and no. errors. Word defines whether the typographical error is for the word *the* or for other words. No. errors defines how may typos are present in the line of text (0, 1, or 2).

Accuracy and RTs can be computed separately for trials with errors on *the* and for trials with other word errors. Proofreading accuracy can be calculated by comparing the number of space bar presses made on each trial with the No. errors associated with that trial. Use the formula described above in the results section to calculate the three subject error scores. To compute the amount of time spent proofreading the passage, total up the RTs for the trials with "SC" error codes.

Representation of Meaning

Experiment 16
Priming in Item Recognition: The Organization of Propositions in Memory for Text

McKoon, G. & Ratcliff, R. (1980). Priming in Item Recognition: The Organization of Propositions in Memory for Text. *Journal of Verbal Learning and Verbal Behavior*, **19**, 369-386. Reprinted by permission of Academic Press.

Introduction To comprehend a passage of text, the reader must build meaningful representations out of the text. Most cognitive theories propose these representations are structured as propositions, which are defined as the smallest basic unit of meaning that could still be true or false. Connections between propositions are built up during reading by sharing an argument. Two illustrations of this structure are shown below.

The youth stole a car.
The car sideswiped a pole.
The pole smashed a hydrant.
The hydrant sprang a leak.
The leak sprayed water.
The water flooded the flowers

Propositions:

P1	STEAL, YOUTH, CAR
P2	SIDESWIPE, CAR, POLE
P3	SMASH, POLE, HYDRANT
P4	SPRING, HYDRANT, LEAK
P5	SPRAY, LEAK, WATER
P6	FLOOD, WATER, FLOWERS

Propositional connections:
    P1——P2——P3——P4——P5——P6

Connections between nouns:
N1	N2	N3	N4	N5	N6	N7
YOUTH	CAR	POLE	HYDRANT	LEAK	WATER	FLOWERS

Table 4. Illustrates a linear propositional relationship in a passage of six sentences of text. P1, for example, consists of two arguments (YOUTH, CAR) which are related by (STEAL). P1 is related to P2 by way of one of their shared arguments (CAR).

These diagrams illustrate three principles about models of propositional relationships: (1) that propositions are the units by which meaning is represented in memory; (2) that propositions are organized according to relative importance and topicality; and (3) that propositions are connected by sharing arguments. This study examined the third principle, shared arguments, or what the authors called argument repetition.

McKoon and Ratcliff have previously used *priming* to determine how close together two propositions are in memory. Priming is the process by which a word or concept, given as stimuli, activates an associated word or concept, so that the RT to the primed word is faster than with a neutral prime. When the deep structure of a story places propositions closer together, their priming effects are stronger than when they are further apart. McKoon and Ratcliff argued that the organizational structure of human memory can be examined using a priming paradigm with RT to measure the approximate distance between two propositions in memory.

> If the representations in memory of the meanings of these paragraphs correspond to the structures built by the argument repetition rule, then the relative amounts of priming between the concepts should be predicted by the relative distances between the concepts in the diagrammed structures. (p.372)

> The businessman gestured to a waiter.
> The waiter brought coffee.
> The coffee stained the napkins.
> The napkins protected the tablecloth.
> The businessman flourished documents.
> The documents explained a contract.
> The contract satisfied the client.
>
> Propositions:
>
> | | | |
> |---|---|---|
> | P1 | | GESTURE TO, BUSINESSMAN, WAITER |
> | P2 | | BRING, WAITER, COFFEE |
> | P3 | | STAIN, COFFEE, NAPKINS |
> | P4 | | PROTECT, NAPKINS, TABLECLOTH |
> | P5 | | FLOURISH, BUSINESSMAN, DOCUMENTS |
> | P6 | | EXPLAIN, DOCUMENTS, CONTRACT |
> | P7 | | SATISFY, CONTRACT, CLIENT |
>
> Propositional connections: 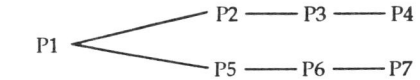
>
> ```
>          ┌── P2 ── P3 ── P4
>    P1 ──┤
>          └── P5 ── P6 ── P7
> ```
>
> Connections between nouns:
>
> ```
>                    N2 ────── N3 ────── N4 ────── N5
>                   WAITER    COFFEE   NAPKINS  TABLECLOTH
>           N1  ──┤
>       BUSINESSMAN
>                   N6 ────── N7 ────── N8
>                 DOCUMENTS CONTRACT   CLIENT
> ```

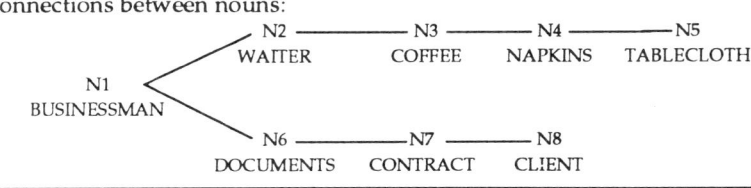

Table 5. Illustrates a branching relationship between propositions in which two lines of connections are formed in the story. Notice that P1 and P5 can be quite close in meaning (deep structure) even though they are relatively further apart in the sequence of the story (surface structure).

Method

Forty-eight right-handed undergraduates served as subjects. Subjects were presented with two paragraphs at a time, after which they were shown 12 words from each paragraph and 12 new words, and asked to say whether each word had been in one of the preceding paragraphs. Some words were primed (preceded by another word from the same paragraph), and some were unprimed.

Paragraphs were of several sorts. In *linear* (Table 4) and *switching* (Table 5) paragraphs, distance between words in the deep propositional structure (how far apart they were in the diagram) exactly corresponded to distance in surface structure (how far apart they were in the story). In *branching* paragraphs this was not the case. In *schema* and *nonschema* paragraphs, every proposition was connected to every other proposition; however, in schema paragraphs connection strength was affected by subjects' previous knowledge of the situation described. There were 144 paragraphs total, presented in two sessions.

There were 48 linear, 16 switching, 48 branching, 16 schema, and 16 nonschema paragraphs.

Results and Discussion

Linear paragraphs showed the expected effects of propositional distance ($F=10.402$, $p=.002$). There was concern that this effect might have been due to previous propositional connections. Switching sentences ruled out this possibility by switching the position of two propositions for half the subjects. These subjects also showed the expected significant distance effects ($F=3.806$, $p=.054$). In both of these paragraph types, propositional distance is confounded with surface distance; this is not the case for branching paragraphs. For these sentences, there was a significant effect of propositional distance ($F=7.081$, $p=.002$).

By diagram, schema and nonschema paragraphs have the same propositional connections; however, schema paragraph should be affected by previous propositional strengths. If the theory is true, differences in priming strength should appear between these two types of paragraphs. This result was found, with marginal significance; non-schema paragraphs showed equal priming strength between all propositions, while schema paragraphs showed greater strength between schema-supported connections ($F=3.249$, $p=.074$) (the authors suggest the marginality of the significance may be due to the small number of these types of paragraphs used).

These results support the theory and the proposed construction of propositional structures.

Running the Experiment

The first experiment of McKoon and Ratcliff is presented here. This experiment is fairly large with over 500 stimuli, but only 16 paragraphs are included.

Data Analysis

There are five trial codes: paragraph, word, surface distance, meaning distance, and direction. Paragraphs are defined in five ways (linear, branching, schema, nonschema, and none--for the foil words which were not presented). We did not include a "Switching" paragraph, which was another form of a linear structure designed as an additional control by McKoon and Ratcliff. Words are defined as foils, primed, or unprimed. A prime is positioned either through a surface or meaning (deep) structural relationship to the target word; so primed words have an additional variable for definition. Surface dis(tance) or meaning dis(tance) are both defined as close, far, or medium. Finally, words which are primed through surface structure have one more definition variable called Direction. When the prime is presented in the story before the target word, then direction is defined as forward, otherwise the prime is backward.

Experiment 17
Semantic distance and the verification of semantic relations

Rips, L., Shoben, E., & Smith, E. (1973). Semantic distance and the verification of semantic relations. *Journal of Verbal Learning and Verbal Behavior*, **12**, 1-20. Reprinted by permission of Academic Press.

Introduction

Early in the study of semantic memory, two different models were proposed: network and set-theory. Network models assumed that words were independently represented in memory and connected by a complex network through which relationships between words were defined. For example, the sentence *A robin is a bird* is represented by two units *(robin* and *bird)*, the connection between them *(is a)*. Set-theory proposed that semantic memory is organized into overlapping sets of elements, where the elements could be exemplars or attributes of the concept expressed by the sentence.

When a person recalls semantic information, some memories take more time to recall than others. For example, people can verify that *A robin is a bird* faster than *A robin is an animal*. To explain this difference, researchers proposed that *robin* and *bird* are semantically more closely related than *robin* and *animal*, a phenomenon described as the semantic distance between them.

Each model of semantic memory had a different explanation for semantic distance effects. Network models proposed that the connection between robin and bird is more direct than between robin and animal, and so the time it takes to verify a sentence is proportional to the number of connections required to link the words. Set models proposed that verification requires a search through a set of elements. The size of the set determines how long the process takes. Because the set of birds in semantic memory is smaller than the set of animals, verification times will differ.

Nevertheless, both explanations for semantic distance effects share a common assumption. Each model proposes that semantic memory is organized to reflect the categorical structure of our language. Both models predict that it will take more time to verify a relationship between items that cross categorical boundaries than for items represented at the same structural level. Because a *robin* is an item in the subset of *birds,* and *bird* is an item in the subset of animals, then to verify that a *robin is an animal* will take longer than to verify that a *robin is a bird*.

In this study, Rips, Shoben, and Smith reported that semantic distance effects do not always occur when items cross categorical boundaries. In one case when the category was *mammal* instead of *bird* the effect was reversed.

Methods

Subjects were 12 undergraduate students, six of each gender. Subjects were presented short sentences with a subject and noun predicate. The predicate nouns were category names *(car, vehicle, bird, mammal, animal)* and subject nouns were items in one of these categories (e.g., *Dodge, robin, bear*). Because *car* is a subset of the *vehicle* category, and *bird* and *mammal* are subsets of the *animal* category, sentences using *car, bird,* or *mammal* as a predicate were referred to as level 1 while sentences using *animal* or *vehicle* were referred to as level 2, reflecting the number of categorical boundaries to be crossed when verifying the relationship between subject and predicate nouns. Fifty-three percent of the sentences were true and 47 percent were false out of 142 total. The words *bird, mammal, car,* and *vehicle* were used equally often in true and false sentences.

Subjects were instructed to determine whether each sentence was true or false, and to press the appropriate button, responding as quickly as possible without making any errors. A warning light appeared two seconds before each sentence. The sentence then remained until the subject pressed a button.

Results and Discussion

The mean reaction times for the correct "True" responses are presented in Table 6.

Predicate Nouns Level 1-Level 2	Level 1 Predicate Noun RT	Level 2 Predicate Noun RT	RT Difference (L1 - L2)
Bird - Animal	1307	1456	149
Mammal - Animal	1371	1283	-88
Car - Vehicle	1268	1380	112

Table 6. *RT comparisons for the different types of predicate nouns.*

Results in Table 6 showed that RT to level 1 nouns was faster than to level 2 nouns (F=12.08, P<.01), and the interaction between categories and levels was also significant (F=9.15, p<.01). Semantic distance effects were seen for *vehicle* and *animal* but the effect was reversed for the category *mammal*.

These inconsistent results suggests that other factors affect the structure of semantic memory besides linguistic categories. Other research showed that word frequency, or how often a word is used, also plays a critical role in the organization of semantic memory (see the next experiment for one example). In this case *animal* is a more common word than *mammal*, which helps to account for the reversal of the semantic distance effect.

Running the Experiment

The first experiment of this study is presented with the categories of *car* and *vehicle* eliminated. The 1971 stimuli for these categories were no longer likely to be recognizable to the average student. This removal reduced the number of trials to 66.

Data Analysis

Trials have three codes: verity, level and category. Verity defines whether the trial statement was true or false. Level defines the level of relationship between the subject and predicate noun in the sentence (L1 or L2). Category defines the whether it was a bird or mammal being categorized as animal.

> **Experiment 18**
> *The occurrence of clustering in the recall of randomly arranged associates*

Bousfield, W. (1953). The occurrence of clustering in the recall of randomly arranged associates. *Journal of General Psychology*, **49**, 229-240. Reprinted with permission from the Helen Dwight Reid Educational Foundation. Published by Heldref Publications, 1319 Eighteenth Street, Washington, DC, 20036-1801. Copyright 1953.

Introduction

During the 1950s and '60s many psychologists provided dramatic evidence that people are not passive learners simply forming associations between stimuli, but take an active role to find ways to make the information they are learning more memorable. One of the classic studies of this kind was conducted by Bousfield. In a previous study he noticed a tendency among subjects to cluster related items during free recall of word lists. For example, in a list of birds, *hawk, eagle, vulture,* and *duck, turkey, chicken, goose,* may be clustered together. In this study Bousfield presented subjects with unrelated lists of words to see if during recall they would to organize their answers in categorical fashion.

Method

Subjects (125 students) were verbally presented with a list of 60 two-syllable nouns. There were 15 words from each of four categories: *animals, names, professions,* and *vegetables.* Words were balanced for frequency of occurrence. Words were presented in a single random order to all subjects, at a rate of three seconds per word. Three seconds after the last word had been read, the signal was given for subjects to begin writing down as many words as they could recall (this was not a surprise memory test). They were given ten minutes to do this, marking a line on the paper at the end of every one-minute interval.

Results and Discussion

Table 5 shows the clustering results for subjects as compared to the clustering in an artificial recall simulation operating purely by chance. The tendency of subjects to cluster well exceeds chance levels.

	1s	2s	3s	4s	5s	6s	7s
Subjects	810	261	164	85	38	18	5
Artificial Exp.	1452	343	87	18	4	1	-

Table 5. Incidence of Single Items and Clusters of Varying Size for Subjects and for Artificial Experiment.

Bousfield proposed two mental factors which together may account for these patterns:

> (a) Habit strength deriving from the reinforcement an item has received both before and during the experiment. (b) Relatedness increment which is a hypothetical increment added to habit strength. An item by virtue of its occurrence adds this increment to the other items to which it is related. (p.237-238)

His ideas have had considerable influence on the research field. Today memorization, almost by definition, means that the information learned has been organized.

Running the Experiment In this experiment the words are presented visually rather than verbally. The free recall portion of the experiment, however, is same. You will need a piece of paper and a pen or pencil.

Data Analysis There are no experimental trial codes for this free recall task, so data analysis must be done by hand. Subjects' responses are organized into 10, one minute time periods during recall. To build a table of item clusters similar to above, review words recalled during each time period and count up the number of words which are in the same semantic category: animal, name, profession, or vegetable. Be sure to check for intrusions, or words which were not on the list. A text file containing the list of words in the experiment is provided to help check for errors.

Experiment 19
An evaluation of alternative functional models of narrative schemata

Yekovitch, F. R., & Thornedyke, P. W. (1981). An evaluation of alternative functional models of narrative schemata. *Journal of Verbal Learning and Verbal Behavior*, 20, 454-469. Reprinted by permission of Academic Press.

Introduction Schemas, or schemata, refer to cognitive structures which organize specific details about the general properties of an object or event. For example, the schema for coffee would include concepts about its, color, taste, and so on but would leave out information about a specific cup of coffee purchased this morning. Schemas organize the abstract information we know about the world in ways which allow it to be efficiently utilized. In this study Yekovich and Thorndyke study how schemas shape our comprehension while reading.

Schemas constrain the interpretation and organization of situations and events in a reading passage. To model these constraints, researchers construct hierarchical tree diagrams which describe the schematic grammar of the story.

High-level story constituents (e.g. theme, resolution) are high in this hierarchy, while plot details are low. Previous studies have shown that people find it easier to remember items high in the hierarchy.

Several different models have been proposed to explain such results. In this experiment Yekovich and Thorndyke examine two differing views on how schemas are utilized during text comprehension.

> [The conceptual view] argues that propositional information is represented in memory in abstract, conceptual form. According to this view, people remember the gist of a text and forget exact wording because the representation in memory is primarily semantic...The lexical view, on the other hand, argues that memory representations maintain lexical and syntactic integrity in memory. Two or more synonymous propositions may be represented and integrated in an associative memory structure that preserves the lexical elements and identity of each. (p. 457)

If the conceptual view is true, then subjects should claim equal recognition for a studied sentence and for a paraphrase of it. If the lexical view is true, then recognition should be much higher for studied sentences.

Method Sixteen high school and college students were first presented with a paragraph, which they were instructed to read at their normal speed. This paragraph had been constructed with a six-level hierarchy, with 1 denoting the highest level story constituents and 6 the details. Subjects were presented with a series of statements for recognition, either immediately or after a 60 minute delay. Recognition test items were of three types: verbatim statements taken from the story (OLD), modified statements with changed syntax and/or synonym replacement (PARAPHRASE), or statements with substituted incorrect details (FALSE). All three types included statements from each hierarchical level. For each sentence, subjects were asked to decide whether it was an old statement, a paraphrase, or new. Subjects were asked to rate their confidence for each answer on a scale of 1 to 5, 1 being "guess" and 5 being "completely confident."

Results Recognition responses were scored as correct for true responses to OLD items and false responses to PARAPHRASE and FALSE items. Mean correct responses and mean confidence ratings (computed by subtracting incorrect item ratings from correct ones and dividing by the number of items) were calculated for each item type.

There was no significant difference in performance between immediate and delayed testing, so data was pooled across retention intervals. Hit rate and confidence rating did not vary significantly as a result of hierarchical level, "consistent with the models that presume no systematic differences in the encoding of story propositions." However, PARAPHRASE items from were rejected correctly more often when they included fewer details and were at a lower hierarchical level.

Analysis of the different items showed that PARAPHRASE items were recognized as new as often as OLD items were judged to be old, supporting the lexical view that memories include syntactical as well as semantic information from the story. Correct rejection of FALSE items also did not differ significantly by hierarchical level, further supporting "the conclusion that subjects encoded both high- and low-level story information."

Discussion These results support a lexical model of memory, but also raise questions about why PARAPHRASEs on more general story concepts are more often correctly rejected than items which are more based on more specific details.

> One possible explanation presumes systematic differences in the semantic content of information at various hierarchical levels. Conceivably, important information may be less constrained in exact content and may permit more alternative surface realizations than low-level information. On a recognition test, this flexibility could lead to higher false alarm rates for important statements. Alternatively, subjects might allocate more processing resources to structural integration of high-level information because of its central role in the narrative organization. Thus, fewer resources would be available to consolidate memory of precise content for high- than low-level information. Whatever the cause, it is clear that people retain much of the surface information from all levels of importance. (p. 466)

Running the Experiment This experiment contains only the immediate test.

Data Analysis Trials are coded for three variables: target type, level min, and level max. Target type defines one of the three kinds of recognition items (Old, Paraphrase, or False). Level min and max define the hierarchical level of the item. Minimum and maximum values are needed because some items were within a range of level values.

Two responses are coded for each trial. The first records subject accuracy on judging the target type. The second records their confidence level.

> Experiment 20
> Remembering: A study in experimental and social psychology

Bartlett, F.C. (1932). *Remembering: A study in experimental and social psychology*. New York: Cambridge University Press. Reprinted by permission of the Cambridge University Press.

Introduction

Early psychologists conceived of learning in terms of the association of stimuli and responses without regard for any participation or influence from the learner. Bartlett had a different view. In 1932 he published a book titled *Remembering* in which he described many memory studies, documenting how the learner took an active role in shaping what they had learned and were able to recall. He was particularly interested in the way people seemed to organize new and meaningful information, adapting the material they learned to existing memory structures which he called *schemas*.

Using a simple recall task, Bartlett attempted to "find something about the common types of change introduced by normal individuals into remembered material with increasing lapse of time."(p. 63) His observations were not measured or quantified under experimental conditions, and in some cases his study took place over a time span of more than ten years. Nevertheless, his ideas have been very influential to modern cognitive psychologists who study schemas and memory.

Methods

Subjects in this experiment were told to read a brief story translated from a North American folk-tale. Each subject was instructed to read the story twice at their own normal reading speed. Bartlett then asked his subjects to write down their recollection of the story 15 minutes after the two readings. Bartlett also asked the subjects to reproduce the story again after an uncontrolled interval of time, varying from a few hours to, in one case, almost 10 years. Many subjects reproduced the story several times at progressively longer intervals.

Results and Discussion

The independent variable is time elapsed from the reading to the attempt at reproduction, while the dependent variable is the accuracy of reproduction. Bartlett described the subjects' recollection of the story as a function of time. He reported instances of phenomena such as the substitution of familiar objects like "boat" for the less familiar "canoe." Bartlett also reported at length on how subjects dealt with the supernatural element in the story. The original story was from a culture very different from that of his subjects, who were 1920s British college students, and he reported on how their own cultural biases affected recollection.

Some of Bartlett's observations and conclusions are summarized as follows:

1. It again appears that accuracy of reproduction, in a literal sense, is the rare exception and not the rule.

2. In a chain of reproductions obtained from a single individual, the general form, or outline, is remarkably persistent, once the first version has been given.

3. At the same time, style, rhythm, precise mode of construction, while they are apt to be immediately reacted to, are very rarely faithfully reproduced.

4. With frequent reproduction the form and items of remembered detail very quickly become stereotyped and thereafter suffer little change.

5. With frequent reproduction, omission of detail, simplification of events, and structure, and transformation of items into more familiar detail, may go on almost indefinitely, or so long as unaided recall is possible.

6. At the same time, in long-distance remembering, elaboration becomes rather more common in some cases; and there may be increasing importation, or invention, aided...by the use of visual images.

7. In all successive remembering, rationalization, the reduction of material to a form that can be readily and "satisfyingly" dealt with is very prominent.

8. Or, again, rationalization may deal with details, explicitly linking them together and so rendering them apparently coherent, or linking given detail with other detail not actually present in the original setting.

9. In the latter case rationalization has three forms:

    (a) The given material is initially connected with something else—usually with some definitely formulated explanation—and treated as a symbol of that other material. Eventually it tends to be unwittingly replaced by that which it has symbolized.

    (b) The whole rationalizing process is unwitting and involves no symbolization. It then tends to possess characteristics peculiar to the work of the individual who effects it and due directly to his particular temperament and character.

    (c) Names, phrases and events are immediately changed so that they appear in forms current within the social group to which the subject belongs.

10. There is evidence of delay in manifest change, transformations being foreshadowed weeks, or perhaps months, before they actually appear. (p.93-94)

Running the Experiment

In the study presented here, the subjects are only explicitly asked to reproduce the story once, after 15 minutes. Following Bartlett's method, students may wish to examine their written recall of the story for the behavioral patterns that Bartlett described.

Data Analysis

Bartlett's procedure does not allow a formal statistical analysis. However, you may want to look for some evidence that supports or contradicts some of

Bartlett's conclusions.

> **Experiment 21**
> *Context-independent and context-dependent information in concepts*

Barsalou, L.W. (1982). Context-independent and context-dependent information in concepts. *Memory & Cognition*, **10**, 82-93. Reprinted by permission by the Psychonomic Society, Inc.

Introduction   Barsalou proposed that two types of properties are associated with concepts. Context-independent properties form the "core meanings of a word" and are activated whenever the word is accessed from memory. Context-dependent properties are activated only in the presence of a relevant context. Take, for example, the word 'bear'. Some context independent (CI) properties of 'bear' could include 'is furry', or 'can be dangerous'. The sentence "The bear caught pneumonia," could activate context dependent (CD) properties like 'can be sick' or 'has lungs'. These are properties which 'bear' does indeed have but which would not be activated without proper context. In a series of experiments, Barsalou attempted to determine if words possess one, the other, or both of these types of properties.

He presented subjects with concept-words in sentences, followed by properties which may or may not belong to the word. If they do, the properties may be either CD or CI. His theory predicted that response time would be faster to CD properties when the sentence is relevant, while context should not affect reaction time to CI properties.

Methods   Data was collected from 18 students participating for pay or class credit. Subjects initiated each trial by pressing a button. For 6 seconds, they were shown a sentence which started with the word "The," followed by an underlined subject noun, and a statement about that noun (i.e. "The seagull ate a fish."). The subject would read the sentence aloud. A property would then appear, which either was or was not true of the underlined noun (i.e. "can fly"), and the subject made a true or false button press judgment.

There were 21 practice trials and 60 test trials. Half of the test trials were "true;" of these, half were CD and half CI. CD and CI relations were confirmed in a separate association test with different subjects. Three types of CD and CI sentences were constructed. For each property, two sentences (one related, one unrelated) had the same weakly related subject ("The banana was peeled" verses "The banana was put in the basket.") The control sentence had a highly related subject and an unrelated predicate ("The bowl collect dust on the shelf.")

Results and Discussion Latencies for correct "true" trials are shown in Table 6.

	Predicate Relation						
	Control		Unrelated		Related	
Condition	L	%E	L	%E	L	%E
Context-Independent	1335	11	1113	0	1145	3
Context-dependent	1098	1	1404	11	1259	3

Table 6. Average Latencies and Error Rates per Subject for Correct True Trials.

Latencies did not differ between the two types of CI sentences (F<1). However, latencies were shorter for related than for unrelated-context CD items (F = 5.97, p<.025). Also, for unrelated-context sentences, CI items had lower latencies than CD items (F = 22.13, p < .001).

> These data indicate that context had no effect on the CI items but had an effect on the CD items. More specifically, related contexts did not increase the priming of properties when the subject noun was highly related to the target property. However, related contexts did increase the priming of properties when the subject noun was weakly related to the property ...These data are consistent with the distinction between CI and CD properties. (p. 86)

Running the Experiment There are three counter-balanced versions of Barsalou's first experiment. Each student should be assigned to only one, but all students should first run the practice session.

Data Analysis Each trial has two code types: context and relation. Context defines if the context is dependent or independent (CD or CI). Relation defines the noun predicate relationship (unrelated, related, or control).

Experiment 22
Facilitation in recognizing pairs of words: Evidence of a dependence between retrieval operations

---

Meyer, D. and Schvaneveldt, R. (1971). Facilitation in recognizing pairs of words: Evidence of a dependence between retrieval operations. *Journal of Experimental Psychology*, **90**, 227-234.

Introduction A variety of factors can affect a person's ability to recall semantic information. Earlier studies showed that high frequency words, that is, words which are commonly used, can be recalled faster than low frequency words. In this study, Meyer and Schvaneveldt examined the effect of the association between two words on recall time. They hypothesized that words which are semantically related could "prime" each other, making recall faster.

Methods Twelve high school students were the subjects of this study. They were shown two letter strings (a list of letters which may or may not be a word), one appearing over the other, and asked to decide if both strings were words. One-fourth of the string pairs were semantically related words (e.g. BREAD-BUTTER), in which the lower word was "the first or second most frequent free associate given in response to the first." One-fourth were semantically unrelated word pairs (e.g. BREAD-DOCTOR). One-third were word-nonword pairs, and one sixth were nonword pairs. Nonwords were formed by replacing at least one letter of a common English word with another to form a pronounceable string (e.g., MARK is transformed to MARB). Subjects were presented with four blocks of 24 test trials each. There were a total of 16 nonword pairs, 32 word-nonword pairs (half with the nonword on top, half with it on the bottom), 24 pairs of associated words, and 24 pairs of non-associated words.

For each trial, subjects were briefly presented with a warning "READY" signal. A fixation box then appeared. After one second the stimulus pair appeared in the box. Subjects then pressed the appropriate response key.

Results and Discussion "Yes" responses were significantly faster for pairs of related words than for pairs of unrelated words ($F=20.6$, $p<.001$). "No" responses were significantly faster, for word-nonword pairs, when the nonword was on top ($F=171.7$, $p<.001$). Error rate for word-nonword pairs was significantly higher when the word was on top ($F=18.9$, $p<.005$). Error rate for nonword pairs was significantly lower than that for word-nonword pairs with a nonword on top ($F=5.5$, $p<.05$).

The results of this study demonstrate that semantically related items have a "priming" effect on each other. The presentation of a related word can make it easier to recognize and recall its semantic partner.

Running the Experiment The first experiment of this study is presented and shortened. There are two blocks, each of which contains 16 nonword pairs, 32 word-nonword pairs, 24 pairs of associated words, and 24 pairs of non-associated words.

Data Analysis Trials have two codes: type and relation. Type defines the four different letter string pairs (word/word, nonword/nonword, nonword/word, word/nonword). Relation defines if the word pairs are semantically related or unrelated.

The Experiments

> Experiment 23
> The organization and activation of orthographic knowledge in reading aloud

Glushko, R. (1979). The organization and activation of orthographic knowledge in reading aloud. *Journal of Experimental Psychology*, 5, 674-691. Copyright (1979) by the American Psychological Association. Reprinted with permission.

Introduction

Early reading models had two parallel pathways for processing text. The phonologic route used spelling-to-sound rules of the language to determine pronunciations of unfamiliar words. Since the rules which were applied were fixed, words with irregular pronunciations (e.g., yacht) would be "regularized" when encoded in the phonologic route. The direct route determined pronunciation by accessing lexical memory. The pronunciation of irregular words would be processed accurately in this pathway so long as the word was known. Pseudowords (or pronounceable nonwords; e.g., mave) always would be processed in the phonologic route. Each route was considered independent of the other. Text was thought to be processed in both pathways in parallel, but the direct route was considered to be faster and so took precedence.

Glushko wondered if two routes were really necessary. He hypothesized that the direct route could process pseudowords by analogy, building a pronunciation by examining how other known words with a similar orthographic structure were pronounced. If the direct route could make such inferences, Glushko reasoned that pseudowords that had orthographic neighbors which only had regular pronunciations would be faster to pronounce than pseudowords that had irregular orthographic neighborhoods because extra time might be needed to resolve the conflicts. The dual-route model would show no difference in pronunciation latencies, since both pseudowords would be processed in the same phonologic pathway.

To test this idea, he compared pronunciation latencies for words with both regular and irregular pronunciations to pseudowords with regular and irregular orthographic neighborhoods. He predicted that latencies would be longer for the irregular words and pseudowords.

Methods

The twelve subjects were all native speakers of English with no speech or hearing impediments.

The four types of stimuli were generated from a set of 43 monosyllabic irregularly-pronounced words (e.g. deaf). Regular words were chosen that differed from the source irregular word by only one letter. (e.g. dean). The initial consonant of each was then changed to generate the irregular and regular pseudowords, respectively. This resulted in a set of 172 experimental stimuli. One hundred additional stimuli were used as fillers.

Each trial began with a fixation, which remained on the screen until the subject pressed a button, at which point the letter string appeared. Subjects were instructed to pronounce this string as quickly as possible while still remaining accurate. Trials were presented randomly, except that each string differed by at least two letters from the one previously presented.

Results and Discussion

Strings were pronounced significantly faster if they were words as if they were regular (F = 6.40, p<.05 for words, F = 16.53, p<.05 for pseudowords).

Stimulus Type	Example	Correct Pronunciation Latency (msec)	Error Rate
Regular Word	DEAN	589	1.9
Exception Word	DEAF	618	12.2
Regular Pseudoword	HEAN	617	6.2
Irregular Pseudoword	HEAF	646	21.7

Table 7. Pronunciation Latency and Error Rate

His most striking result was that pseudowords with irregular neighbors (e.g., HEAF) take longer to pronounce than regular pseudowords (HEAN). This result supports a more flexible model for applying the two pronunciation mechanisms than those previously suggested and led to new single-route models of reading.

Running the Experiment

Glushko's first experiment is presented here, but without the filler trials. You will need to use a computer that can take microphone input for the Macintosh. The Windows/PC version only takes RT keyboard responses as a lexical decision task.

Data Analysis

Trials are coded for category and regularity. Category defines the word type (word or nonword). Regularity defines if the letter string was regular or an exception.

> *Experiment 24*
> *A ROWS is a ROSE: Spelling, sound and reading*

Van Orden, Guy C. (1987). A ROWS is a ROSE: Spelling, sound and reading. *Memory and Cognition*, **15**, 181-198. Reprinted by permission by the Psychonomic Society, Inc.

Introduction

Dual-route reading models propose that words can be decoded in two ways: you can recognize the word on sight (direct route) or you can sound out the word using spelling-to-sound rules of the language (phonologic route). In early versions of this model there was little cross-talk between the two processing pathways, so that direct access to lexical memory would provide the correct pronunciation of a word without any phonological mediation. Furthermore, since the direct route was faster than the phonologic route, reading by directly accessing memory was considered only to involve the processing of visual or orthographic information about text. Since skilled readers have extensive sight vocabularies, and so presumably use the direct route when reading, most theories considered phonology to be important for beginning readers but not used by skilled readers.

In this study Van Orden shows that phonological mediation can occur in skilled reading. He employed a categorization task in which subjects judge whether a target word is a category exemplar. For example, "Is PAIR an exemplar of the category FRUIT?" According to Van Orden:

> The phonological mediation hypothesis predicts that false positive categorization errors should occur as a function of the phonological similarity of a stimulus foil to some category exemplar. Accordingly, when the target word is a homophone foil such as ROWS, its phonological representation should strongly activate the lexical entry of the category exemplar ROSE prior to word identification. If so, the homophone foil ROWS will tend to be misidentified as the flower ROSE. (p.182)

Therefore, when a subject is asked to say whether or not the word is an exemplar and to read the word aloud, if the subject answers "YES, ROZ" for the category A FLOWER then, the subject has activated phonological information about the word.

Dual-access theories would predict categorization errors both when foils sound like category exemplars and when they are spelled similarly to category exemplars. This prediction was tested using homophone foils that varied in the degree to which they were spelled similar to their sound-alike category exemplars. Target foil MEET (for the category A TYPE OF FOOD) is very similar in spelling to MEAT. Target foil ROWS is less similar in spelling to ROSE. If an orthographic representation is used directly in word identification, then the likelihood that this process will be misled by orthographically similar foils should be a function of the number of orthographic characteristics that they share with a category exemplar. Thus, MEET is more likely to be mistaken for MEAT than ROWS is to be mistaken for ROSE.

Method

All twenty subjects were native speakers of English and had normal or corrected-to-normal vision. Each subject received a block of 50 practice trials followed by 122 experimental trials. Each trial began with the presentation of a category name centered above a fixation point. After 1.5 sec the fixation point was replaced with a word. After 500 msec, both were replaced with a pattern mask. Subjects were instructed to press one button if the word was an exemplar of the category, another if it was not.

Of the experimental trials, only 16.4% were trials in which the target words were homophone foils. This percentage was intentionally low to avoid inducing processing strategies by the presence of a high percentage of phonologically ambiguous stimuli.

The order of presentation for all trials in the practice task and the filler trials in the experimental task was the same for all subjects. However, for each subject, the key trials containing homophone or spelling control foils were assigned randomly to predetermined presentation slots separated by one, two, or three filler trials. During the experimental trials each subject sees 20 homophone foils (10 similarly spelled, e.g., MEET, and 10 less similarly spelled, e.g., ROWS), 20 corresponding spelling controls (e.g., MELT and ROBS), 41 real category exemplars (e.g., LILY for A FLOWER), and 41 obvious non-exemplars which were chosen not to be systematically similar in any way to category exemplars.

Results and Discussion

This experiment had two independent factors: 1) the manipulation of homophony and 2) the manipulation of orthographic similarity. The percentage of false positives was the only dependent measure. Results are shown in Table 8.

	Similarly Spelled Foils		Less Similarly Spelled Foils		
	Mean	SE	Mean	SE	Mean
Homophones	29	6.9	8	2.9	18.5
Spelling Controls	5	3.1	1	1.0	3

Table 8. Percentage of False Positive Responses to Homophone and Spelling Control Foils.

The Experiments

The mean false positives for homophone foils (MEET or ROWS) were significantly greater than for the spelling controls (MELT or ROBS), [t(9) = 3.90, p < 0.05, for subjects, and t(19) = 3.64, p < 0.05, for items].

Also, the percentage of false positives to similarly spelled homophone foils such as MEET (29%) was significantly greater than that to less similarly spelled foils such as ROWS (8%) [t(9) = 3.71, p < 0.05, for subjects, and t(9) = 2.27, p < 0.05, for items].

These results support a reading model in which both orthographic and phonological representations influence the process of word identification for skilled readers.

Running the Experiment Van Orden's first experiment is presented here with only 98 experimental trials.

Data Analysis Trials are coded for three variables: word type, filler type, and similarity. Word type is defined as homophone, spellin(g), filler, and practic(e). Homophones and spelling types are further defined by the similarity variable as similar or less si(milar). Fillers are further defined by the Filler type variable as exempla(rs) or nonexem(plars).

Reasoning

Experiment 25
Pragmatic reasoning schemas

Cheng, P. & Holyoak, K. (1985). Pragmatic reasoning schemas. *Cognitive Psychology*, **17**, 391-416. Reprinted by permission of Academic Press.

Introduction When people reason about realistic situations, Cheng and Holyoak proposed there are three methods available. First, they could deduct a set of abstract, logical rules for building inferences that could apply to a variety of different contexts. Second, they could draw on previous experiences to help form a judgment about the specific situation. Or third, they could use pragmatic reasoning schemas, which are generalized sets of rules defined in relation to classes of goals that could help them prediction the outcome in a given situation.

To test their ideas Cheng and Holyoak use a modified version of the Wason selection task.

> In this task subjects are informed that they will be shown cards that have numbers on one side and letters on the other, and are given a rule such as, "If a card has a vowel on one side, then it

has an even number on the other." Subjects are then presented with four cards, which might show an "A," a "B," a "4," and a "7" and are asked to indicate those and only those cards that must be turned over to determine whether the rule is true or false." p.391

Other studies have shown this task can be very difficult, but when the task is rewritten to include common items in a realistic context, such as stamps on letters, it can be much easier. Some researchers have proposed that people do poorly due to fallacies in their logical reasoning or because they have not had any other experiences like this task which could guide their judgment. Cheng and Holyoak, however, argue that Wason task is difficult to do because people prefer to reason using pragmatic schemas, and the Wason task does not provide information which can be readily organized into a familiar schema from which they could form logical inferences.

Methods   Subjects were divided into two test groups. The first included 88 students from the University of Michigan, and the second included 82 students from the Chinese University in Hong Kong. Each group was given two selection tasks, one involving letters and postage, the other involving immigration cards and diseases. Both are situations which pose a simple Wason task to be solved.

There were two versions of each task. One simply presented the task without explanation. Another version provided subjects a pragmatic schema by explaining, in a few additional sentences, a rationale behind why this task was being done. Each subject received the rationale version of one task and the no rationale version of the other.

Results and Discussion   The Hong Kong group already was familiar with the postal task, since a similar law was actually in effect in Hong Kong before the experiment. The Michigan group, however, had no previous experience with this particular type of postal regulation. According to the pragmatic schema hypothesis, all subjects should perform better on the rationale tasks than the no rationale tasks because the rationale should activate a pragmatic reasoning schema. The exception to this pattern of results would be the Hong Kong students on the postal task. Since they were familiar with a similar postal regulation, a pragmatic schema already existed and providing a rationale would given no additional benefit.

The results provided clear support for their hypothesis. The Hong Kong group did well on both versions of the postal task, but in all other cases, subjects scored about 30% better on the rationale version of the tasks.

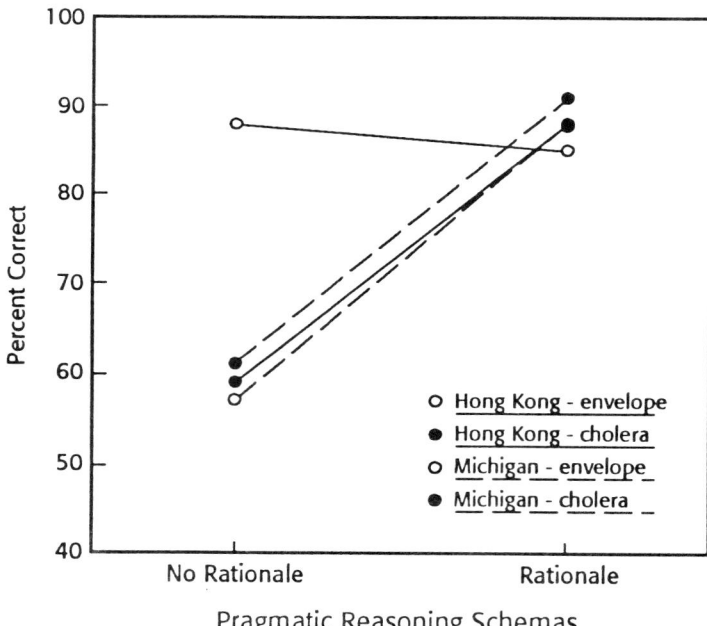

Figure 17. Percentage of subjects who solved the selection task correctly in each condition as a function of provision of a rationale.

Running the Experiment There are two counterbalanced versions of Cheng and Holyoak's first experiment; each student should be assigned to one. In the original study subjects wrote down their answers with an explanation. In this on-line version subjects choose one of the fifteen possible responses.

Data Analysis One trial code (schema) identifies whether a rationale was provided or not.

The Collected Data File

SuperLab Pro records all the responses provided by the subjects, whether correct or not. These are saved in a tab-delimited text-only file. In addition, SuperLab Pro for Windows will also record "non-responses", i.e. events that have a time limit but to which the subject did not respond.

```
John Doe
Letter Rotation
 9/23/87    20.07
```

Trial Name	Trial #	Event #	Response	Error Code	Reaction Time	letters	orientation	F and B	R and L
instructions	1	1		C	1146				
1	2	2		C	1446	L	150	front	right
2	3	3		C	763	F	90	front	left
3	4	4		E	1746	F	30	back	right
3	4	4	b	SC	2596	F	30	back	right
4	5	5		C	913	R	150	front	left
5	6	6		E	1880	L	90	back	right
5	6	6	b	SC	2763	L	90	back	right
6	7	7		E	2246	L	180	back	right
6	7	7		E	4430	L	180	back	right
6	7	7	b	SC	5113	L	180	back	right
7	8	8		E	913	R	60	back	right
7	8	8	b	SC	1896	R	60	back	right
8	9	9		C	1429	F	30	front	right
9	10	10		C	563	L	60	front	left
10	11	11	b	C	879	R	0	back	right

The above snapshot of the results file has been formatted for presentation's sake; the results file you obtain will be plain text.

The first field is the trial name. The second field is the trial number (order). The reason for this redundancy is because a trial number is easier to process with statistical software than a name.

The third field is the event number, followed by the subject's response. In the snapshot above, responses are either blank (space bar) or the character B.

The fifth field contains an error code. SuperLab Pro generates an NR for no response (Windows version only), C for correct, an E for error, or an SC for self-correct, meaning the subject responded previously with a wrong answer then responded with the correct one. The error code is followed by the reaction time, in milliseconds.

A varying number of fields follow the reaction time; these are the code values attached to the trial. The number of fields depend on how many codes you have defined.

Glossary

ANOVA is the abbreviation for the term **analysis of variance**. It is a statistical technique for examining the variability in a set of data to determine whether the difference in scores is due to random fluctuations or caused by one of the **factors** in the study.

blocks are groups of **trials** in an experiment. They are used to organize the **conditions** of the experiment in a uniform way. Trials can be organized in several ways: they can be randomized within a block; they have a fixed order; or they can be randomized with constraints, such that each block only contains a certain set of trial **conditions**.

condition refers to one of the combinations of **independent variables** used in the experiment. For example, in an experiment with two variables that each have two **factors**, there would be four experimental conditions.

contralateral means the opposite side of the body with reference to a particular anatomical location. For example, the right hemisphere of the motor cortex in the brain controls the contralateral side of the body, in this case the left-side.

correlate is a **variable** which is related to another variable in such a way that a change in one is associated with a change in the other. For example, a correlate of high blood pressure is heart disease. Variables do not necessarily have a "cause-and-effect" relationship. Their association may be incidental as the result of other intervening variables. For example, a correlate of eating ice cream is accidental drowning. An increase in one is associated with an increase in the other, probably because of their common association with warm summer weather.

counterbalance is a procedure for balancing the order in which **trials** or **blocks** are presented during an experiment to counter practice and fatigue effects. Over the course of an experiment, **subjects** can grow tired of or become more skilled in performing the experimental task. Arranging the trials in a particular order can distribute the conditions of the experiment uniformly to control for these effects. Sometimes subjects receive different counterbalance orders. Practice and fatigue effects can still be eliminated by averaging performance across this set of subjects.

dependent variable is the behavior being measured in the experiment. **Subject** performance is dependent upon the **conditions** of the independent variables. When graphing *encoding*   the relationship between them, the dependent variable is always plotted on the y-axis and the independent variable on the x-axis.

encoding   means the processing of a **stimulus**. Encoding can be unconscious and require little attentional effort, or it can require conscious effort.

event   is part of a **trial**. Trials are made up of event sequences. Events can present **stimuli** to a **subject**, wait for specific time periods with no stimuli presentation, or can record subject responses.

F=46.4, p<.001   are statistical terms associated with ANOVA calculations. The term F=46.4 is reporting the value of a ratio of the **variance** between experimental conditions and the variance found within conditions. Under properly controlled conditions, the within-condition variance is caused by random fluctuations between **subjects**, whereas the between-condition variance is caused by random factors plus the effects of the **independent variables** on subjects' task performance. If the independent variables have influenced the **dependent variable**, the between-condition variance (the term in the numerator of the F-ratio) should be larger than the within-condition variance (the term in the denominator), and the F-ratio will be larger than 1.

How big does the F-ratio need to be before we could claim that the independent variable had a statistically significant effect? The size of this ratio dependents on the number of **factors, conditions,** and subjects in the study. Random factors out of the experimenter's control also can influence the size of the F-ratio. Therefore, with the number of experimental factors, conditions, and subjects taken into consideration, statistical significance is determined by calculating the probability that a given F-ratio would have occurred by chance. This probability value (labeled p) is reported along with the F-ratio. Psychologists usually adopt a probability threshold value of .05. This means that if the probability is less than 1 in 20 that the F-ratio could have occurred by chance, the results of the experiment are considered to be statistically significant.

factor   is a term used to describe the different types of **independent variables**. The term is synonymous with **variable**. For example, a study may be designed to examine the effects of age and sex on short-term auditory memory. Age and sex are factors or variables. Factors can be further organized into subgroups called **conditions**. For example, ages may be grouped into conditions of young, middle age, and elderly.

fixation   refers to a visual **event** used to begin a **trial** involving visual displays. The fixation usually is used to direct a **subject's** attention to the location where information will be displayed during the next trial event.

hemifield   refers to a part of the visual field only seen by one cortical hemisphere. For human vision, the left half of the visual field is processed first by the right cortical hemisphere, whereas the right visual field is processed by the left cortex.

interaction   means that **conditions** of at least two **independent variables** interact in different ways. For example, consider a study with two factors, age (old & young) and sex (male or female) measuring RT. Hypothetical results showed an effect for age (younger were faster) and an interaction between age and sex (men were faster than women but only in the younger group).

Interactions are most easily seen when graphing the relationship between dependent and independent variables. The plot of two or more lines that describe a subjects' performance on different variable conditions usually will cross over one another when there is an interaction between independent variables.

independent variable   is one of the **factors** manipulated by the experimenter in the study to determine its effect on the **dependent variable**.

intercept   refers to a point on the graph where the relationship between the **dependent** and **independent variable** intersects the y-axis. It usually describes a threshold point for one of the independent variables.

ipsilateral   is the opposite of **contralateral**. This term means the same side of the body with reference to a particular anatomical location.

lesions   refer to damage which has occurred to part of the brain.

letter strings   are a list of letters which do not necessarily makeup a word. Words can be letter strings too, but of course, *WXJY* is not a word, but still a letter string.

lexical decisions   is an experimental **paradigm** in which a subject decides whether a letter string is a word.

mean   is a measure of central tendency in a set of data, usually calculated by the arithmetic average of a set of scores from a group of subjects or scores from a set of trials under the same conditions.

mean latencies   is the average response delay. Timing usually begins at the start of the presentation of the target event and stops when the subject makes a response.

paradigm   describes a set of experimental tasks used to measure a subject's behavior.

parietal lobe   is part of the cortex in the brain located to the side and near the back of the head.

posterior   means toward the back of the head.

predicate   is the part of a sentence which expresses something about the subject of the sentence.

probe	describes a type of **stimulus** used prior to recording a subject's response that may influence the response in a predictable way.
reaction time	is a type of **dependent variable** that measures the time it takes for a subject to respond. Usually a button or key-press is recorded, but sometimes the vocal onset latency, or time to utter a response, is measured.
semantic	refers to the meanings of words.
slope	is the angle of deflection of a line on a graph which plots the relationship between the **independent** and **dependent** variables.
statistically significant	means that in a statistical test, the probability of the result being a chance occurrence is less than 1/20, or .05.
stimulus	or the plural **stimuli** are experimental events in which provide the subject information.
subjects	are individuals who give informed consent to participate in an experiment.
target	is a **stimulus event** for which the subject makes a response.
trials	are sequences of events that present stimuli and record **subjects'** responses in an experiment.
variable	is synonymous with **factor**. It refers to an attribute under study that can assume more than one value.
variance	is a measure of dispersion in a set of data.

Index

Abelson, R. P.	27	intercept	26, 33, 67
ANOVA	8, 23, 33, 65	ipsilateral	10, 11, 67
attention	9	Jonides, J	9
allocation of	6	knowledge structures	27
feature integration	17	Lavie, N.	12
Barsalou, L.W.	53	lesions	9, 67
Bartlett, F.C.	51	McKoon, G.	41
Black, J. B.	27	memory	
Bousfield, W.	47	autobiographical	27
Broadbent, D.E.	13	episodic	22
Cheng, P.	60	high-speed scanning	24
clustering	47	knowledge structures	27
Codes		propositions for text	41
attached to trials	63	serial search	24
Collected data		mental extrapolation	29
save	63	mental rotation	30, 34
concepts, information in	53	Meyer, D.	55
contralateral	9, 10, 11, 65	narrative schemata	49
counterbalance	15, 28, 62, 65	Navon, D.	37
Craik, F.	22	orthographic knowledge	56
dichotic listening	13	parietal lobes	9, 67
Dilollo, V.	20	Pinker, S.	29
Dixon, P.	20	Posner, M.	9
Eriksen, C.	6	predicate	46, 54, 67
Finke, R.	29	probe	26, 34, 67
Friedrich, F.	9	Pylyshyn, Z.	34
Gelade, G.	17	Rafal, R.	9
Gellman, L.	30	Ratcliff, R.	41
Glushko, R.	56	reading	58
Gregory, M.	13	reading aloud	56
Healy, A.	39	reading units	39
hemifield	10, 66	reasoning schemas	60
Hochberg, J.	30	recognition	41
Hogben, J.	20	recognizing pairs of words	55
Holyoak, K.	60	Reiser, B. J.	27

Response	
collected	63
Results File	(See Collected data)
retention of words	22
retrieval operations	55
Rips, L.	45
Save	
collected data	63
Schvaneveldt, R.	55
semantic	68
categorization	24
category	48
distance	45, 47
information	50, 55
memory	45, 47
relations	45
Shoben, E.	45
Smith, E.	45
sound	58

spelling	58
Sternberg, S.	24
Stroop, J.	14
temporal integration	20
Thornedyke, P. W.	49
Treisman, A.	17
Tsal, Y.	12
Tulving, E.	22
Uninstall SuperLab	2
Van Orden, Guy C.	58
verbal reactions	14
visible persistence	20
visual	
perception	37
processing	12
Walker, J.	9
Yeh, Y	6
Yekovitch, F. R.	49